# PROPHETIC RECONSTRUCTION
The Remnant's Response

Evangelist Amber Brown
Author of Rise To The Mission

Copyright © 2021 by **Evangelist Amber Brown**

All rights reserved. No part of this publication may be reproduced, distributed or transmitted in any form or by any means, including photocopying, recording, or other electronic or mechanical methods, without the prior written permission of the publisher, except in the case of brief quotations embodied in critical reviews and certain other noncommercial uses permitted by copyright law. For permission requests, write to the publisher, addressed "Attention: Permissions Coordinator," at the address below.

**Evangelist Amber Brown/Rejoice Essential Publishing**

PO BOX 512

Effingham, SC 29541

www.republishing.org

Unless otherwise indicated, scripture is taken from the King James Version.'

Scripture quotations marked (NIV) are taken from the Holy Bible, New International Version®, NIV®. Copyright © 1973, 1978, 1984, 2011 by Biblica, Inc.™ Used by permission of Zondervan. All rights reserved worldwide. www.zondervan.comThe "NIV" and "New International Version" are trademarks registered in the United States Patent and Trademark Office by Biblica, Inc.™

**Prophetic Reconstruction/Evangelist Amber Brown**

ISBN-13: 978-1-956775-08-2

Library of Congress Control: 2021923877

Isaiah 58:12 says, "Those from among you shall build the old waste places; You shall raise up the foundations of many generations; And you shall be called the Repairer of the Breach, The Restorer of Streets to Dwell In."

Now is the hour to Rebuild! Repair! And Restore!

# ACKNOWLEDGMENT

I would first like to give honor to God, who is the head of my life. I can do nothing without Him. It is in Him that I live, move, and have my being. I thank Him for all that He has done and continues to do through me and for me. He gets all the glory out of my life. I want to thank my children and family for always supporting me in my endeavors and loving me through it all. I give honor to my spiritual covering and Shepherds, Bishop Ron Webb and Dr. Georgia Webb, for always believing in me and helping to pave the way for my success in the Kingdom of God. The teaching and leadership that I sit under and absorb from has helped to bring me where I am today in my maturing relationship with Jesus Christ. I would like to thank both Prophet John Veal and Prophetess Kimberly Moses for supporting me and being a very special part of this book in this season of my life. To all those who have sown into my life in many different ways, my prayer is that the Lord will reward you for being a blessing to me. I honor those who have helped me grow spiritually and those that have poured into me over the years. May God pour into you double!

I pray that the words you are about to read activate your spirit and the giftings on the inside of you. You are charged and challenged to get up and do the work God has called you to do in these last days.

Never Count Yourself Out; Count Yourself Able in Jesus' Name!

# TABLE OF CONTENTS

ACKNOWLEDGMENT.....................................................................v
FOREWORD................................................................................vii
INTRODUCTION...........................................................................1
CHAPTER ONE:     The Process of Reconstruction for the Church........................................................5
CHAPTER TWO:     Seasonal Prophecy........................................12
CHAPTER THREE:     The Turning Point of Re-Entry for The Church...........................................17
CHAPTER FOUR:     The Action of Alteration............................23
CHAPTER FIVE:     Unlocking Destiny One Word At A Time...............................................................28
CHAPTER SIX:     The Shadow of Me Is Not My Reality in Prophecy.......................................35
CHAPTER SEVEN:     Provoking the Prophetic.............................41
CHAPTER EIGHT:     The Kingdom Awakening............................46
CHAPTER NINE:     The Renewal of The Watchman.................52
CHAPTER TEN:     The Breaking of Fertile Ground.................58
CHAPTER ELEVEN:     The Playground of Christianity..................63
CHAPTER TWELVE:     Take the Band-Aid Off...............................70
ABOUT THE AUTHOR..............................................................77

# FOREWORD

We are living in the last days and among a wicked and perverse generation. So much has happened in the prophetic community where we see prophets against one another. Some aren't truly hearing the heart of the Father but speaking from their flesh. As a result, many are wounded, confused, and shun prophetic ministry. " Prophetic Reconstruction The Remnant's Response," written by Evangelist Amber M. Brown, is the solution the prophets need. Her book is like spiritual CPR and will stir up prophets to focus on the One who died on the Cross for their sins. God is using this book as a reminder to stay humble. As you read the pages in the book, you can sense the urgency of the Holy Spirit to repent, get right with God, and stay focused on what we are called to do because time is short. "Prophetic Reconstruction" comes straight from the throne of heaven and is designed to help heal wounds and divides in the Body of Christ. Evangelist Amber M. Brown's penmanship brings life to the reader who may have gotten weary to "rise to the mission" and be about our Father's Business. I highly recommend this book to those who don't know their purpose, sitting on the sidelines, the broken, and weary. Also, every prophetic minister needs to have a copy of this read in their arsenal to keep their heart pure and motives right in God's sight.

***Prophetess Kimberly Moses***
*Publisher, Founder, and Author of Rejoice Essential Network*
*Florence, South Carolina*

In this book, Evangelist Amber Brown challenges our thinking and causes us to refocus on the new wineskin. This book is a Prophetic Recall and will certainly charge us to push the restart button moving forward. The Revelation in this book brings a new meaning to Isaiah 43, "Behold I will do a new thing." This is the kind of book you can interview and take all over the world to jumpstart God's people. Amber is a noted Author as well as Co-Author of Shaking Hands with Wisdom, and Sought after speaker that challenges you to leadership and equips you to Rise To The Mission in these last days. For every 5-Fold Ministry gift and anyone entering into ministry, this is a must-read. I highly recommend all faith-filled believers should read this book if they are unsure what direction to take. I believe this book will help guide you to the prophetic future.

**Bishop Ron Webb**
*Author of Leadership From Behind The Scenes/*
*Christian T.V. Show "Leadership From Behind The Scenes"*
*Senior Pastor*
*Mt. Calvary Powerhouse Church*
*Poplar Bluff, Missouri*

Many of today's prophetic ministries need spiritual rehabilitation. They are in desperate need of a makeover. We have seen churches that have been decimated by the pandemic of 2020, some to the point of never opening their doors again. But there is a remnant rising in this hour that will lay hold to the promises of God in this season and refuse to let go! They are mission-minded as they pursue His mandate. Their fervency will provoke others to jealousy, causing some to embrace a new prophetic paradigm. In this season of reconstruction, prophetic warriors such as Amber M. Brown are rising up! They are laying claim to the truths of God and responding to His clarion call. Amber's desire is to show you how to re-enter not just a building, but become part of a spiritual reconstruction crew! This crew is a remnant of people that will take the church to an entirely new level in God! They will deconstruct the plans of the enemy and construct the ministry of the Most High!

In her new book, Prophetic Reconstruction: The Remnant's Response, Brown displays a spiritual boldness and insight regarding the current state of the church. She diagnosis the "dis-ease" that has crept into the prophetic part of the ecclesia and gives remedies for the various ailments that seek to deconstruct it. Brown literally speaks to the architecture, seeking to produce a possible change that could alter its current design.

I believe this book is significant. It pulls no punches when it comes to the truth. The author makes a clarion call to the reader; urging them to an action of alteration; be the change that they want to see. Her use of Scripture is lavish, further cementing the points made within this literary work. Brown's love for God's house and its citizens is quite evident here. She wants the church to reset, regain, and refocus in order to awaken the Kingdom within them as never before!

Amber M. Brown's latest work is a love letter to the Body of Christ. In Ephesians 4:15, the Bible admonishes us to speak the truth in love. This is exactly what she does in "Prophetic Reconstruction: The Remnant's Response". This book is primarily for those that desire change. It's for those cognizant of the time they have left on earth and truly want to accomplish more for the Lord. It's for those who seriously want to get their prophetic gift moving in an entirely brand new way. I am excited about this message to the Body from Amber! I believe that it has the potential to provoke change in those that truly receive it. I believe that this writing will be a welcome addition to other reading material that you've gathered in your prophetic war chest.

**Dr. John Veal**
*Senior Pastor-Prophet*
*Enduring Faith Christian Center*
*Chicago, Illinois*

# INTRODUCTION

Leadership is not about the position; it's about rising and becoming the product of your mission. The road less traveled tends to be the roughest because not many have conquered it, but the greatness of those that have made it to the end is that they live to tell it. Beloved, you can have what you believe, and the Remnants are Emerging in this last hour and their response to what God is doing will change the face of Discipleship as we know it. Increasing in strength and growing in stature, God's Spirit is pouring out on all flesh who are hungry and thirsty for a move of God, and fear of what's coming in the natural world cannot be what hinders you spiritually! You can no longer live on the fence of God's Word. We cannot pursue both temporal and eternal in the Kingdom. It is like holding on to two horses galloping in opposite directions. Sooner or later, you must let go of one. It is never comfortable or natural to treasure the invisible over the visible, the promises of God over the promises of the world, the things that will not be fulfilled until the return of Christ over the things the world says we can have right now. Yet, the Scriptures tell us that the only time security comes is from abandoning the illusion of control and surrendering ourselves unswervingly to the person and the purposes of God. When you let go of the world, you must learn a completely new life forcing you to meet the original you, the person you used to be before you allowed all the conforming of the world to take place in you.

God is prophetically reconstructing the church. His Word in you is the best part of you! Now is the time where we must get back to our first love and our reason for continuing to wake up every morning. I wonder how many of us have been held back because we are too scared to be bold in the face of adversity. You have so much potential, but that is all it will be until your mind gets free! This is the hour to find your voice. Period!! Your inability to get over the past has paused your anointing! It has emptied your gas tank! It has taken your resources, but your past does not define who you are; it just merely helps give meaning to your future. So, the person that you are destined to be is the person that you decide to be! People of God, it is not about where you've been, but it's about where you're going. I always say your past just adds a little spice to your God-given flavor. We will make it through these changes, and we are going to grow and flourish like never before, but first, we must face the truth of our present before stepping into our future.

This has been the worst time for many mentally and physically but the best time for those who truly live by faith! If you want a life full of results, you must live a life full of faith.

**Hebrews 10:38 (KJV) reminds us that, "Now the just shall live by faith."**

Just meaning righteous, steadfast, and faithful. As a believer walking through these trying times, I have found myself envisioning an hourglass, and as I watch the sand drop, I ask myself, "as many that are dying hour by hour because of doubt and unbelief, God is there yet one in this hour that will RISE for you?" During this pandemic, my prayer has been that the Lord would send forth laborers into His harvest because the mission is great, the mission is getting bigger, and it must still go forth.

**The Bible says in Luke 10:2 (KJV) that "the harvest truly is great, but the labourers are few."**

This is truly a time of transition for the body of Christ into transformation. The Remnants are emerging and coming out of those hidden places that have kept them comfortable and complacent for far too long.

*You are not what you go through, but you are everything that you stand for!*

Many contain the gifts and secrets of the Kingdom of God and have no idea they have been called in these last days to the prophetic reconstruction of the church! God is tired of seeing His vision sitting dormant buried inside of a vessel that hasn't been positioned yet with no manifestation of His works, so He has allowed some things to take place in these last couple of years to shake the very core of His creation. Now is the time when we see firsthand the difference between being a hearer of the Word and being a doer of the Word. God's value on Kingdom principles doesn't go down just because of a pandemic. As we start committing to the reconstruction process, we as a church whole will begin seeing the response that we have prayed for so long.

**Spiritual Warfare has been at its highest for the body of Christ, but we must remember that Zechariah 4:6 (NIV) says, "it's not by might, nor by power, but it's by my spirit says the Lord."**

Even though this period of reconstruction has been painful, this process has been for a purpose. God is rebuilding what His church (we as believers) are supposed to look like and should be doing in these last days. Many have fallen to the wayside, and we must do our very best to get them back up, but in the meantime, God is raising up an army that He is building for this specific battle and we will be the ones to pave the way for the future. The circumstances around us have hindered us in certain areas of our lives. Still, it hasn't stopped those who, through it all, have lived consistently, fully persuaded, never forgotten, that no matter what we are going through or seeing happening around us, we must keep going!

There have been many fallen soldiers who must be restructured and trained for the battles ahead. Therefore God's chosen must Rise Up in this last hour and work while it is day because when night comes, no man can work (John 9:4) and the night is coming! God has created you for more, and He has already started sending people into your life for a specific purpose at a specific time to help hold you up. At the same time, the reconstruction takes place, the rebuilding of your heart, the renewing of your mind, and the prophetic injunction that has taken place to dispense the wisdom of good and evil, spirit and flesh.

On this day, God is calling you forth to set your spirit on fire. Jesus rose so that we could too, and now it's time to Rise To The Mission!

*I say the hourglass has just been flipped, so the question is, what are you going to do with the time that you have left?*

CHAPTER ONE

# THE PROCESS OF RECONSTRUCTION FOR THE CHURCH

John 2:19-21 (NIV) says, "To those who sold doves he said, "Get these out of here! Stop turning my father's house into a market!" His disciples remembered that it is written: "Zeal for your house will consume me." The Jews then responded to him, "What sign can you show us to prove your authority to do all this?" Jesus answered them, "Destroy this temple, and I will raise it again in three days." But the temple he had spoken of was his body."

God is rebuilding the church. Not a church building but His people! The church building allows us to assemble in one place, praise, worship, and hear God's Word while being trained and discipled for the work of service in His Kingdom, but many have forgotten that God doesn't stay behind in the building when we leave, but He goes with us wherever we go.

*The Holy Spirit spoke to me while I was writing this book and told me that many believers are waiting for their next "fix" or "pick me up" on Wednesday and Sunday like an addiction. They are addicted to what church looks and feels like but not addicted to what the church should look like in them!*

People of God, where we look, we will go; and what we behold, we become. Change has called and now the question is, are we going to answer the call? The call of not making it about the position but becoming the product of our mission.

You cannot leave here with unfinished business! Jesus is about to turn the keys and God will be opening doors to His Kingdom, to endless possibilities, and a life that can never be destroyed. Generation after generation, there have been times of uncertainty and change as to what the future holds, but despite obstacles and challenges, you are still here today by the grace of God for the process of reconstruction.

*There are things yet to be revealed to you and through you! Promises still need to be held! Wisdom still meant to be dispersed! Giftings still need to be accessed, utilized, and manifested on earth!*

I want you to say, "I might have made some mistakes but today I decided to start making some moves. Moves that only God has the strategy for!" This is a Call to Action. God is preparing a meal and everyone reading this book is being seasoned with the Spirit of God and by the time you leave this earth, you will leave with the fullness of the meal if you sit and eat it every day of your life. In John 14:26, Jesus tells us that the Holy Spirit will teach us all things and will remind us of everything He has said to us.

So, in the process of reconstruction of the church, we must first understand that we have **The Promise of The Holy Spirit**. The fact that Christ comes to us through the Holy Spirit should cause us to respond quickly. And we know that because He left the Holy Spirit with us, we know that there is a job to do FOR US ALL! Verse 12 says, "Greater works will you do because I go to the Father," and the greater things He discussed is converting people to Christ and performing miracles on earth through His Spirit in us.

I see much wisdom in the earth. The great age of the earth is getting older but still is consumed with the Spirit of God more than ever before. God's wisdom and design brings life in old and low places, especially dark places, to show the world that humility looks up. During the process of reconstruction for the church, we must humble ourselves and remember to look up! Jesus had to come from a high place to walk in a low place, but He found His treasure in that low place. His treasure in earthen vessels! In humility unto God, we can produce a power outwardly to reach others by an inward motivation and power to perform it because of the rebuilding in you by the Holy Spirit. We must be about our Father's business while He is restructuring what we will look like in the future. I think more and more people get comfortable and then lose sight of the end goal.

> *Every day Satan comes to steal your destiny! To kill your Purpose! And to try to abort God's Power and promise within you! But Shout, "the Devil is a Liar!" In the ring of life, I got Jesus as my tag team partner. So, I know that I can take a hit but keep on swinging!*

So, we know that during the process of reconstruction, we have the **Promise** of the Holy Spirit working through us and now we get to **the Manifestation of the Spirit.** In I Corinthians 12, we can read the different manifestations of the Spirit. If the attributes of God will be manifested in His people, then the attributes of Satan will also. When we allow the Holy Spirit and the giftings operate in us, we can detect Satan and evil works because God gives us the advantage of the law of double jeopardy. This means that Satan, "an invisible creature" can be addressed through a visible creature," which is us. We can be seen but Satan and his demons cannot be seen in the natural sense but can be seen spiritually with discernment. As God rebuilds you, the enemy will come for you but don't allow fear to stop you! This is when we get to the Power in the unveiling. If we have an expectation of God, we will always receive the manifestation of His presence! Victory is not by accident; it's by choice, and the Unveiling of God is in operation among us.

*God is here now activating the person of Jesus Christ, the presence of Jesus Christ, and the power of Jesus Christ through His people to His people!*

In the Old Testament, God spread a cloud for a covering by day and fire to illuminate by night, but now we have His Spirit living on the inside of us. We may not always understand, but the miracle in living the reality of Christ is in our movement in His Word through the shadows of darkness. Darkness cannot drive out light, but light always drives out darkness. The Bible says in Genesis 1:2-3 (NIV), "Now the earth was formless and empty, darkness was over the surface of the deep, and the Spirit of God was hovering over the waters. And God said, 'Let there be light,' and there was light." This just shows it is mandatory for the Holy Spirit to be with us in operation before miracles can take place. God brought the dead to life and illuminated it and lit it up, and the best part of all, He put us in it!

This is why we cannot become complacent in where we are now in the flesh that we compromise who we are in the Spirit. As children of God, we are joint-heirs with Jesus Christ. While on earth, you must know who you are and what you possess! Jesus is the entrance and there is a great big Kingdom out there full of doors awaiting to be unlocked and the Holy Spirit is with you to lead and guide you into all truth in the Kingdom while on Earth. There is purpose in you that has never left, and no man can stop! A purpose that says, "God who began a good work in you will complete it until the day of Jesus Christ" because it is God at work in you giving you the will and the power to achieve His purpose.

During this process of reconstruction for the church, age is just a number. We are all still on assignment breathing the breath of resurrection, being formed in our mother's womb for a specific birthing into this world at just the right time to fulfill promises upon promises of God's Word to come alive within us.

*Jesus has walked the sands of the desert and has traveled the bluest of waters. He knows exactly what is ahead for you.*

God has every tool, every resource you need to accomplish your mission. This world is full of "I'll believe it when I see it" mentalities, but I know there are some people that can say like David in Psalm 37:25 (NIV), "I was young and now I'm old, yet I have never seen the righteous forsaken or their children begging bread." Why do things like Covid-19, Opioid Epidemics, Suicide, Racism, Injustice, and Politics take over and distract the saints? Because Satan wants those things to distract us from the real fight, which is Satan himself, and when the believers stay distracted, it leaves an open door for the enemy to keep us divided. But this is where the **Power in the Unveiling** takes place. Our sin, our shortcomings, our inability to meet our true selves in the Spirit, which is the mirror of ourselves in Christ, is what has kept us comfortable. Speaking excuses and producing no good fruit to leave with the next generation. Therefore being a contributor to the problem and not becoming part of the solution.

*Beloved, we will have what we say and live out the choices that we make.*

I heard an analogy one time and it said, "Sin is like a jail cell, nice and comfy with doors wide open. There's no need to leave until one day your time runs out and the doors shut and it's too late." This is true, but it's never too late with God. God is now rebuilding and restructuring what His people are supposed to be and look like for what He has planned. Now that the veil has been removed, we can go to the Father and have another day to get it right before our time runs out.

*"But since we have such hope, we are very bold. For this day, we know it is only through Jesus Christ that the veil is taken away. But when one turns to the Lord, the veil is removed! Now the Lord is the Spirit and where the Spirit of the Lord is, there is Freedom. And we all, with unveiled faces, reflect the glory of God being transformed into the same image from one degree of glory to another, which comes from the Lord, who is the Spirit. When Christ came, He went through the greater and more perfect tabernacle that is not made with human hands. He did not enter by means of goats and calves, but He entered the Most Holy place once and for all by His own blood obtaining eternal redemption! How much more than will the blood of Christ who through the eternal Spirit offered Himself unblemished to God, cleanse our consciences from acts that lead to death so that we may serve the living God while still living on this earth!"*

We are called according to His purpose, and you will receive the promised eternal inheritance in Heaven while also operating in the promises through the Holy Spirit on Earth.

*Remember, for every trial, God has your triumph! For every attack, God has your answer! For every tear, God has your garden! For every Setback, God already has a Victorious Comeback planned for you!*

The reconstruction of the church has begun and when the time of God is birthed in the Spirit; it's a beautiful thing. We will start seeing the Remnants arise like never before, and as they start rising, we must pray for them that their faith will fail them not during this season of Prophetic Reconstruction.

CHAPTER TWO

# SEASONAL PROPHECY

Mark 2:22 (NIV) says, "And no one pours new wine into old wineskins. Otherwise, the wine will burst the skins, and both the wine and the wineskins will be ruined. No, they pour new wine into new wineskins."

In this chapter, we must be reminded that if we are going to accept the new that God has for us in this next phase of our destiny, we must let go of all the old ways of thinking, doing, and being. God is very intentional about our growth and development with everything in our lives because He knows that pouring new revelation on an old mindset is never going to produce change in one's life, but will end up falling to the ground, never to be planted in good soil therefore not accomplishing anything. Our mind and demeanor must be in a specific state that is conducive to bear witness with the Word of God. God sent an angel to John who bore witness to the Word of God and the testimony of Jesus Christ. Since this is so, how much more does God send in your life to bear witness with the Word that God gives you?

**The Bible says in Revelation 1:3 (NIV), "Blessed is the one who reads aloud the words of this prophecy and blessed are those who hear, and who keep what is written in it: for the time is at hand."**

We must meet the need that the vision requires for the specific time that we are in. The Bible says there was a time when we were yet sinners, but Christ died for us because He knew that our season of restoration was coming. We just hadn't come to that point yet. You see, God knows what you need and when you need it, and He allows you to discern what is coming. The problem with the church is that we see the problem coming, but we are waiting for someone else to speak up and do something, not accepting the fact that God was telling us to do it the whole time! People of God, we have no control over what God wants and expects out of us in any season of our life. We are just told to surrender in whatever season we are in to receive what we need in that season.

We are to be living sacrifices. What that tells us is that every season we must sacrifice something. Whether it be our time pouring or our time receiving, we are to be partakers of what God has for us in that moment of our life. Every season we are learning and growing but not every season looks the same. If the sick never see the physician, then the sickness remains. If the teacher never teaches the student, then the student will never learn. If the Prophet never takes time to be silent and listen prior to the test, then the words that come out of their mouth during the test will not be the correct answer for the right questions and seasons of another's life. You will not hear accurately from God if you are not spiritually where you need to be. There is a lot of noise, but prophets, you are waiting for the small whisper.

The Bible shows us that there will be many seasons of our life that we must look in the eyes and face. Whether a time of birth and death or weeping and joy, God's timing is perfect and will grow your faith as you are forced to wait and trust in God through the process. Then when that specific time of breakthrough comes and the shift from weeping to joy flows out of you, only God can get the Glory out of your life. We go from Faith to Faith! Glory to Glory! Strength to Strength! That is why seasonal prophecy is so important. In one season, you may be the one receiving, but then there will be a season that you will be the one pouring out, and you must have the discernment moving forward knowing which season you are in. There will be some people in this chapter of your life that must be reminded and redefined again by God's Word while others reading this book are the ones that God has redefined and are now ready and profitable for the work that must be done RIGHT NOW. Seasonal prophecy in the Will of God for your life is the key that unlocks and shifts you into your next.

*God wants to redefine everything that has been misplaced, mishandled, and misused. Our Kingdom Advantage is this: there are no limits to your living as a Christian who walks jointly with the Holy Spirit.*

This is a very strategic time for the Body of Christ. Because of what has happened, many people have been seasoned with a burden of frustration that will not go away on the level that they are in. It will require moving beyond the mindset they are in now to birth what is needed to fix the problem where the frustration began. God is sending new people into your life for seasonal prophecy. Seasonal prophecy has a time limit and never lasts! So, you must know what season you are in. And we must get this revelation. Prophecy is meant to come to pass but there's never only one prophecy for a person; there are many strategic smaller things that must happen before that specific prophecy may come to pass. Many words are spoken specifically to a person, whether at the younger stage of their life or when they are older. All are meant to manifest at different times depending upon where we are spiritually, physically, mentally, and emotionally.

**I John 2:24-25 (KJB) says, "Let that therefore abide in you which ye have heard from the beginning. If that which ye have heard from the beginning shall remain in you, ye also shall continue in the Son and in the Father. And this is the promise that he hath promised us, even eternal life."**

We are to keep in our hearts what we heard from the beginning so that the prophecy can continue to live through us and in us before we see the manifestation of it. Faith is defined as the substance of things hoped for and the evidence of things not seen. The Bible speaks about many of God's people having to live by faith and believe His Word before it could ever come to pass. **A prophecy must vacation in your mind first and then take residence in your heart.** The world was framed by the Word of God alone and it was possible because the Word was God and was with God and then He spoke it because He believed it would become alive as soon as He instructed it to.

Now, God's people, having the Holy Spirit on the inside of us, already have the being of God in us; therefore, whatever we believe and whatever resides in us makes us who we are to the point of speaking a thing and already knowing that it will become alive, because God's Word is alive and active! We hear it all the time. If you want the Word to work, you must work the Word! Esther was told that if she remained silent in the time that she was in that her family would perish, but she came into her royal position and assignment at the appointed time. She never gave up or lost her faith. She remained obedient and ended up saving an entire generation because she soaked when it was time to soak and then spoke when it was time to speak. Noah believed the Word of God and built the ark even though he didn't know when God's Word would come to pass. The Word resided in him because God was with him and when God is with us, we know that He will perfect that which concerns us until the coming of Jesus Christ. Sara received strength from God to conceive and deliver a child because of Abraham's prophecy.

Here is a revelation. There are people connected to you that will birth things pertaining to your prophecy that God gave you and it is all a part of God's will. You may not always be the one in the forefront of the vision, but God will bring to pass your prophecy through those connected to you and the great thing about it is it still comes back around to you. Prophecy may not always come how you think it should, but it always comes right and on time, which is why discernment is important because many people are speaking, but not all of them are speaking the truth. There is much deception in the air.

*Untamed and Untrained spirits are speaking out with no covering, no leadership, no accountability and expecting to make a difference only to realize they are the ones causing problems and then making more work for the true prophets that are emerging!*

If the spirits don't line up with the Word of God, then it is not of God. There must be faith in God's Word and obedience to His will. These two things are inseparable, just as unbelief and disobedience are inseparable. So, as you watch, listen, and receive, make sure that it lines up with what God is showing you. Remember to always be ready in season and out of season because who knows, maybe you have come to the Kingdom for such a time as this and the generations to come are waiting on you to take your rightful place as God's mouthpiece to bring healing and deliverance to all who have an ear to hear what thus saith the Lord.

CHAPTER THREE

# THE TURNING POINT OF RE-ENTRY FOR THE CHURCH

Isaiah 55:8-11 (NIV) says, "For my thoughts are not your thoughts, neither are your ways my ways, declares the Lord. As the heavens are higher than the earth, so are my ways higher than your ways and my thoughts higher than your thoughts. As the rain and the snow come down from heaven, and do not return to it without watering the earth and making it bud and flourish, so that it yields seed for the sower and bread for the eater, so is my word that goes out from my mouth: It will not return to me empty but will accomplish what I desire and achieve the purpose for which I sent it."

I want to start this chapter out by saying that life is never just butterflies and rainbows, and at times it can seem like the highest waves are crashing in on you and making you feel like you have nowhere to go. Like you can't even see the land nearby, and you must swim and swim until you find the shore so that you don't drown, unsure of when you will stand on solid ground again. But there comes a time in your life when you look around and understand that the only control you have in your life is the ability to choose to do what you have to do to live in these moments, or you can give up and allow your life to pass you by. Are you choosing to swim and swim and never stop swimming until you make it to where you need to go?

This is what the turning point of re-entry is all about. Take a moment and think about those just re-entering the workforce after being released from prison. Also, think about the addict choosing to start over and begin their road to recovery but not having support. Lastly, think about the Christians whose faith is being tested in these last days having to come to terms that the world as we know it will never be the same. They still have the choice to either continue moving forward doing what is right or letting go of everything that they have lived for to join in things that now they are willing to die for.

Many are entering a brand-new way of life after COVID-19 with many questions but not able to find many answers. Others, while being quarantined, realized how much trauma they were carrying, triggered by the pandemic, and have reached out for help. Some churches have closed, never to open their doors again, while others are still thriving. Healthcare workers are being fired or finding other employment because of their choice not to get vaccinated, while others got it because they have a family to provide for. Extra assistance is being given to families who need it, which are prayers answered for them. In contrast, others have used it to continue staying unemployed but having all their bills paid for by the system, which has encouraged them even more not to work.

Single mothers who are working and trying to teach their children to work for what they have and not live off the system are now not getting the help that they need because they make just over the required amount, while others who can work but don't work are taking from those who do. Fathers who have fallen are now beginning to get back up again. Instead of giving them resources, a helping hand, or helping them learn to utilize those resources on their own as respectable citizens in their communities, they are forced to start paying child support immediately as they re-enter the world outside the prison walls. If they don't quickly find employment, they go right back to prison, but thank God for the programs that are now coming to life for those who are re-entering the world after being incarcerated. I am trying to give you a picture of why we are where we are today. I have also experienced that just because someone says they are faith based and want to help people doesn't mean their basis is found and built on Godly principles and motives. Men can get back on their feet after release, but the system has made it so hard on them that when they do get out, there's not much hope to see in a world that gives up on others based on poor decision making. But this is when God steps in! So, we are seeing the hand of God act in this time, unlike any other time we have experienced thus far. I believe all this must happen because of the transition that must take place to transform the church as the Body of Christ. God allows these things to happen as a permission slip from His people to move in their lives on earth and cause miracles to take place for His glory to be seen and known on earth. God wants us to change.

*We can't change what we refuse to confront.*

We have been called to higher ground, which is why God has had to shake everything that we thought was holding us up to bring forth a rebuilding of His people. Some people are living in the valley. They have never experienced what it is like living on the mountain top, while many mountain-top Christians have no idea what it's like to fight through the valley because they have been raised in church their whole lives, sheltered, and spoon-fed everything. But here's the thing, there are no victims in the Body of Christ. At one point in my life, I played the victim. To my flesh, I was a victim, but there came a point when I realized what was done to me, I decided to allow it to affect me to the point of losing who I was. It didn't have to; I allowed it to! Forcing myself to live in the valley because I didn't think I could climb the mountain, be free, or have more than what I was used to having. Then as I started walking a different path and met the turning point of re-entry for my life, I saw a life in front of me that I could have, but needed help getting there.

Many of you reading this book are re-entering a territory that you know nothing about and need direction and strength from God. You need a word from God that will move you in the right direction, that will keep you from falling lower and lower into darkness. This is where your faith needs to come in. Many of you are leaders who have lost businesses or Pastors who have lost church members and you are praying and asking, "Where do I go from here?" Listen, God is the God on the mountain, and He is the God in the valley. When you are in the valley and feel like you can't see, His Word will give you the light you need to show you the way and when you are on the mountain top, His Word will give you the mercy and grace needed to hold up others that are not where you are.

To all Leaders and Pastors, there are people out there that have a word of activation for you that God will use in this season of your life because they are on assignment to be a repairer of the breach for you. Just because you are not where you want to be or where prophecy said you would be, God's timing is always the best. So in this season of re-entry, you must make sure to rebuild with Him as your solid foundation so that when the winds come and the lightning strikes, you will be ready!

God has shown us that dry places need to be watered and unfinished business that remains for His people must be accomplished. You must get into position.

*Don't allow a temporary cause to result in a permanent effect.*

You must transition with the changes so that you can be a part of the transformation. While others are prospering and growing, you will still be where you were last year and the year before that and the year before that, never experiencing the all surpassing power of God. You must fight for what really matters.

*Some of you are even waiting for closure, but listen to me. A reason doesn't wipe away the tears. Rejection is a part of your healing and God is using rejection as your redirection in this season.*

Anything you have in your life that keeps you from moving forward today, God is telling you to let it go. Let go of traditions that are not working anymore because in this re-entry process, the old way of doing things is not going to work. Stop allowing things to keep you chained in a prison that only gives you a window to see the Promised Land but never gives you anything to help you get there. But even those that have found themselves in a prison spiritually, God has a plan on getting you out and not just you, but everyone connected to you.

**Acts 16:26 (KJB) says, "And suddenly there came a great earthquake so that the foundations of the prison house were shaken: and immediately all the doors were opened, and everyone's chains were unfastened."**

Once you encounter your turning point of re-entry and completely surrender to God and allow Him to build you for the battle ahead, you will be strong enough to go back and get everyone you had to leave behind because you were then too weak to carry them. God did it for Paul and Silas then, and He can and will do it FOR YOU NOW!

CHAPTER FOUR

# THE ACTION OF ALTERATION

Luke 11:33 (NIV) says, "No one lights a lamp and puts it in a place where it will be hidden, or under a bowl. Instead they put it on its stand, so that those who come in may see the light."

As much as you give God from this day forward, is as much exchange you will receive! Our God is a giver, and gifts are permanently and purposely placed. You may have been sitting on the lies of the enemy before the revival that is about to break forth in you but where God is taking you is a NO SIT DOWN ZONE in the spiritual realm! Some of you have been in the valley long enough and God is sending a wave of breakthrough through the Holy Spirit and all you must do is believe it to receive it. God is breaking through the hearts of His people.

While I was talking to God during my prayer time, He pointed out that many people say words that sound good to the mind, but right now, He needs His people speaking words that penetrate and change the heart! When that happens, then true revival can begin.

*For growth to exist and manifest, we must first speak to what's hidden. If You want change, you must open the door to your soul!*

We all get it wrong sometimes, but we must let God be God in our lives. If God has not been the head of your life and you have allowed the enemy to bring you down and oppress you, then today is your chance to get free! God is a God who never stops moving, moving from one place to another, which requires change, brokenness and surrender in your spirit, mind, and heart to get you to a place you have never gone before.

Reconstruction is taking place because the church (God's people) has lost focus. As a result, the lamp of the body has started to become dim. Luke 11:34-36 (NIV) goes on saying,

**"Your eye is the lamp of your body. When your eyes are healthy, your whole body also is full of light. But when they are unhealthy, your body also full of darkness. See to it, then, that the light within you is not darkness. Therefore, if your whole body is full of light, and no part of it dark, it will be just as full of light as when a lamp shines its light on you."**

God gives us this gospel of light that we may repent, receive forgiveness, and be saved. Do you want to know when revival takes place within you? When you start building an altar. When you step onto the altar of His presence and take action, that is what starts the process of an inner alteration. As we allow the prophetic reconstruction of God's Word to be downloaded in us spiritually through the prompting of the Holy Spirit, we instantly allow God to make alterations within us that will glorify Him and bring heavenly principles into our reach. This will ignite the flame in us just as a flame of a lamp in a room that was dark but now sheds light and overpowers all the power of the enemy.

*There is no force of darkness strong enough to withstand the power of sustained intercession.*

As believers, we must live according to the action of God's Word. Not the action of others or their words, especially if it doesn't line up with the Word of God, and many now have chosen to appoint themselves and chosen to build their own platforms. They are operating with no covering and no accountability for what they say and do. Therefore, while the ears of the people are hungry for words that appeal to their flesh, there goes the enemy causing distraction and division from the presence of God in their lives. God is nowhere in the accolades of fleshly emotion, but He stands firm on the power of allowing your flesh to die so that instead you can live spiritually and bind every enemy that tries to hinder or oppress you.

God is a God of change and restoration. If no one is changing or growing from what you're speaking, then chances are it's not from God. So, where there is no restoration, there is another spirit in operation. Therefore, the Action of Alteration is so vital in this last hour. It is victory that becomes questionable when we put people in the place of God. That is one of the reasons we lose what we think we love or need because it is only what is in the will of God for our lives that will last. Why has a pandemic caused people to stop walking through the doors of the church building? Because where there once was the action of alteration has now become an excuse to stay home and make others get up and do what God had already built and equipped you to do.

The people of God can go to Walmart, work, and travel but can't go worship with other believers?

*There are many temporary pleasures that the people of God have made time for, but very few are willing to surrender those pleasures to permanently impact this world in these last days spiritually.*

But remember that God is no respecter of person so as soon as you're ready and willing to get it right, He is already waiting there with His hand reached out.

**Romans 2:11 (NIV) says, "For God does not show favoritism."**

But you do have a choice.

*You can make the choice to allow the action "the movement of God" to cause a reaction in you in this last hour, or you can continue watching the world pass you by and not be a part of the one passing by!*

It's your heart that needs the Healer, and the alterations and adjustments have already begun the moment you picked up this book. My experience in allowing God to move within my heart got me to where I am today and causes me to continue growing because I am continuing to allow Him to make alterations within me. It is the grace of God that has placed us in this moment for this specific time for the purpose and plan of God, and without allowing Him to work in you, you will never allow Him to work through you.

I want you to understand that the Holy Spirit has no age. God can work through a 5-year-old just like He can work through a 90-year-old. God meets you right where you are, which is why He sent Jesus to die for you so that God could meet us where we were but changed forever where He planned for us to go! So, every action of alteration in your life requires faith. Faith in what? Faith that God has His hands on everything that you're not, right now, but everything that will be after you submit in this season of your life.

Many have become so complacent in the flesh that they have forgotten about who they are in the Spirit. We may not always understand God's ways, but we must respect God's timing. And the time for the Church is right now!

*I remember jumping 10,000 feet out of an airplane and the miracle of that was the fact that I jumped. The faith it took to jump is what got me the experience of landing!*

What is it that you have needed to do but couldn't because you lacked faith? Go write that down so you can look at it down the road after you have accomplished it and remember where God brought you from because of your faith! Now, the moment you lack faith, you know your altar is gone, and when your altar is gone your action of being altered disappears. God will never leave you, but He won't force you, and many of you have died spiritually and need to be awakened and altered so that God can use you and not have to pass you by because of your lack of preparation and alteration.

*Remember, brothers and sisters, a diamond must be altered to its value. A seed is ready and produced only in its own time. A relationship is built and lasts only by trusting the process, and growth will only happen with one allowing God to pluck and groom!*

You must allow God's love and mercy to rebuild your heart so that your response moving forward to the chaos in this world will not be an echo in the streets but an alarm that never goes off for those who have fallen.

*That is what the action of alteration is all about. When you have the light within you, every dark place will never remain around you.*

CHAPTER FIVE

# UNLOCKING DESTINY ONE WORD AT A TIME

Philippians 2:13 (NIV) says, "For it is God who works in you to will and to act in order to fulfill his good purpose."

Because our adversary uses what little time he has left to wear out the saints of God, many have become complacent in the action of salvation, thinking that is all there is for them. Many saints think that salvation alone is all Christianity is and all God expects from us, but the devil is a liar! There is a whole kingdom that we must tap into while still on this earth. There is power on high given to us as Children of God to have what we speak and accomplish all that we put our hands to do. We are not here to wash down the gospel of the Kingdom of God through Jesus Christ; we are here to create, birth, and be fruitful with God's Word in us to cause a sweet-smelling savor that will fill this land and consume everything that God already says is ours for the taking. Our words are to produce change and restructure the very core of what Heaven on earth represents.

Promotion and exaltation are occurring in the spirit realm and the flow and movement of God's Word and presence are conducive for the Holy Spirit to use whoever is willing to say, "yes!" in this moment, and willing to act on that "yes!" in this season. This is the season to jumpstart your faith and ignite your spirit! The Holy Spirit is here to empower us, not enable us to always wait on Him to do everything, but to act ourselves. Some words are meant to be spoken to confirm you, while others must be spoken to release you!

**Romans 12:6-8 (NIV) says, "We have different gifts, according to the grace given to each of us. If your gift is prophesying, then prophesy in accordance with your faith; if it is serving, then serve; if it is teaching, then teach; if it is to encourage. Then give encouragement; if it is giving, then give generously; if it is to lead, do it diligently; if it is to show mercy, do it cheerfully."**

Many have counted themselves out by looking at what's going on around them, but God needs a community of people who will stop giving up and start getting up!

**II Peter 1:3 (NIV) says, "His divine power has given us everything we need for a godly life through our knowledge of him who called us by his own glory and goodness."**

*There is always a time when we are called and then separated for the purpose of preparation.*

And this has been a time of preparation for the church! There is a process to God. He is always many steps ahead of us, which is why we must be willing to unlock parts of us as we walk with Him to get the necessary keys to the next level doors that we come to through our obedience in speaking God's Word and walking in Faith, that God will manifest His Word in your life. For Example: To those who God has already chosen and predestined to steward certain landmarks of

His creation, there is land in your region that is already yours because God already owns it and you have already called it into existence!

**Mark 11:24 (NIV) says, "Therefore I tell you, whatever you ask for in prayer, believe that you have received it, and it will be yours."**

And because God already owns it and you're here changing the atmosphere to create it by speaking the word that is already in you, then one day it shall be yours! It already has your name written all over it but are you truly prepared to handle it right now? Are you in communion with God on a level that every time He knocks on the door to your thought life, will you open it up to Him so that He can show others His glory through you?

You see, there is a sound and a frequency to God. It's like driving a car and turning on the radio station so you can hear it. It comes in really good, loud and clear, but the further away you get, the less the station comes in. The Holy Spirit has seen what has been done in the dark and the people have walked away instead of drawing closer to God. Still, even as God is disappointed in what His people have allowed to happen during these times of calamity, Jesus is interceding for us and praying that we all get it together so that His will may go forth in our lives.

The sin that has been in the lives of many has now caused the station to go out! Doubt has hindered you! Fear has stopped you! Continuing to live in old mindsets has stopped the flow of God, but I know that someone who is reading this right now is saying, "yes, that's me, and I need to make a change!" I know you want to unlock destiny one word at a time with God. I know you want to unlock destiny one action at a time with God. You don't want to miss what God wants to do in you and through you in this season of your life, and your prayer should be, "I'll go Lord! Send me!"

**Isaiah 6:8 (NIV) says, "Then I heard the voice of the Lord saying, "Whom shall I send? And who will go for us?" And I said, "Here am I. Send me!"**

Be someone that God can look upon and say, "Yes that's the one bringing Heaven on earth." This walk is not for the faint of heart, and in order to Rise To The Mission, we must remind ourselves of the responsibility that we have as Ambassadors of Christ.

**Acts 17:28 (NIV) says, "For in him we live and move and have our being."**

We have an example in the Book of Numbers. Moses led the Israelites out of Egypt, but his ego got in the way and cost him the Promised Land. In these last days, we can disqualify ourselves from certain areas of leadership for allowing our flesh to get in the way even if we are saved. We can still hold ourselves back from having a prosperous life on Earth if we do not follow through with what God asks us to do. But what God has for you is for you when you sit down at the table of commitment and eat. Will you be ready for what you get before you walk through the door to destiny?

Moses showed us what not to do. God is showing us that there must be a transition to create and build transformation after this pandemic and it's only going to worsen, which is why we must get better. You cannot pour new wine into an old wine skin. Things will never be the same again, and now we are learning new ways of doing things. This has been a hard time for so many, but we have seen the faithful and we have also seen the unfaithful.

*When times get tough, we can't tuck our tail, run, and hide in a corner. We must face our giants.*

Some have remained steadfast and faithful but feel like they have hit a brick wall. I know some of you during this season of your life have been dealing with some Edom's who are standing at the door to your destiny, refusing to allow you through, but God always finds another way to get you where He wants you to go.

**Exodus 14:13 (NIV) says, "Do not be afraid. Stand firm and you will see the deliverance the Lord will bring you today. The Egyptians you see today you will never see again."**

In Numbers 21, the Israelites came to an appointed time. The Unlocking of their Destiny. That once denied passage is now a "possession of the land." As you read, you'll see that Sihon went with his forces against Israel but ended up running upon his own ruin, and that is exactly what will happen to all of those trying to stop you from entering your doors to destiny. What the enemy meant for evil, God will turn for your good. Every single time! So, there is always success on one side and a learned lesson on the other.

The more the enemy tries to stop you, the more he sets himself up to fail in this last hour. The enemies of God's church often perish by foolish counsel. Instead of making peace with Israel, they chose to start a war and that is what many have done instead of using wisdom and all coming together to figure out how to move forward from here, which is why God is raising up the remnants and now we are responding!

**Decree and Declare:**

*What tried to kill me these past couple of years, I can look at face to face and say, "What killed others will not kill me! What stopped others, will not stop me! Devil, you can't stop me on this road to destiny because God has given me dominion and authority for each door to my destiny and I will unlock them one door at a time!"*

Where chaos is, there is no order and God is a God of order. Therefore, we cannot have trespassers in the Kingdom operating illegally with "Spiritual Revelation," in positions and callings they were never assigned to.

**Proverbs 19:21 (NIV) says, "Many are the plans in a person's heart, but it is the Lord' purpose that prevails."**

I am curious to ask, "where is all the wise counsel?" The coverings for the 5-Fold Ministry normally stood right at the door but now some are nowhere to be found. Some are standing there at your door to destiny with no idea of how to cover you while you're passing through, so now in these last days, God is raising up leaders that will be bold in the face of adversity and not go running when times get tough. If the King would have had wise counsel, I don't believe he would have waged war on Israel and gotten his people killed. This is not a game people of God. There is a responsibility in leadership and in this last hour, we are all walking through different doors designed to meet us where we are and take us where we need to be. God ended up giving Israel success and unlocked their destiny because of obedience.

Unlocking destiny one Word at a time comes with a true calling, separation from the world, and preparation. So, a refusal of one door is an opening for another, and your job is to listen to God and know which one is which as you move forward in this crucial time.

*When time is birthed, we see days, weeks, months, and years.*
*When time is birthed, we see Spring, Summer, Fall, and Winter.*
*When time is birthed, we Rise with the sunrise and we lay with the sunset.*

Your goal now is to know how to be prepared before the shift so when your time comes, you'll know how to handle the Words and the Life that He chose for you!

CHAPTER SIX

# THE SHADOW OF ME IS NOT MY REALITY IN PROPHECY

Isaiah 51:16 (NIV) says, "I have put my words in your mouth and covered you with the shadow of my hand-I who set the heavens in place, who laid the foundations of the earth, and who say Zion, "You are my people."

To ignite our passion would mean that we would need to be in a place of complete surrender to our purpose. Many have lost sight of that because of our human nature wants to lean towards our flesh. It is in the flesh that we die but, in the spirit, we live! The revealing is taking place, but it is never too late for a new beginning. So now that the shadow of God's hand covers us, we do not have to live in the shadow of our past.

Our want for more must become more powerful than the pain that is holding us back. Our reality in God being His children means that we are now made in His image, so the things we have done, the mistakes we have made, are no longer present. We remember them, but we are no longer a part of them! We have not been created to be a stagnant shadow of the past, but God wants to do a new thing.

Many people choose to live in the shadow of who they are because they don't want to change. To heal would mean that we must let go of "it" or "them," but they don't want to give up those things. They want to stay in the comfort of their emotions, but the truth of the matter is while staying comfortable and complacent, we lack the strength to break through the barrier of change and find the solution of escape. We can choose to rise above the shadow of who we have accepted ourselves to be and allow God to come in, clean us up, and cover us. In these honest moments of humility with Him and with self, we spot the very things within us that go so many times unnoticed or ignored. We always ignore what we don't want to face! The Remnants are rising, and they are rising above fear. We must face our fears because they turn into our strengths tomorrow. Today we must face our opponent and that opponent is ourselves! There are some things that you don't want to face, but you must be free. Some people will always be prisoners of their own choices, but you must choose not to be that person.

Christians have become complacent in salvation, that they have created a stagnant shadow of who they are when God says there is a reality that you have yet to see! In Acts 9, Saul humbled himself while on the Road to Damascus. He listened to the voice of Jesus, he acted in the ways of God by prayer and fasting for three days, and he envisioned himself in a different place then, and because of his obedience, he became who God created him to be. Some of you are saved but not fully living the reality of who God says you are and having what God says you can have. It is not enough to just receive salvation. You have benefits as a child of God, which causes you not to live or look like all the hell you have been through.

In this season of your life, God will show you who you are in Him and the authority that you have will be used for His good. There is a reconstruction taking place and it is taking place in you! The prophetic rebuilding of the church will look completely different in these last days. So Saul was the shadow of who Paul really was without Jesus Christ. The dark, the incomplete, the messed up, and flawed part of him, but as soon as he started following Christ, everything changed! He completely changed and even while others still judged him for the things he did in his past, God chose him and made it known to the people that Saul was not the man he used to be. He was now living in the reality of who he really was in Him. Saul had to break barriers and change his perspective to live a life of reality and not darkness.

**Psalm 23:4 (NIV) says, "Yea, though I walk through the valley of the shadow of death, I will fear no evil: for thou art with me; thy rod and thy staff they comfort me."**

So now after reading this, we can see that as we walk in the valley of the shadow of death, we are comforted by the authority we have in God and the transformation of our image to God's image. So now we don't have to walk in the darkest valley in our flesh but we walk in the Spirit! We are not who we used to be brothers and sisters! God's love changed us forever!

Please understand that in this season of prophetic reconstruction, even though you are now made in the image of God, we are still having to live on this earth, which means the more you grow in God, the more you grow in the natural. So, what you see now is not what you get! People like to say that cliché, but I don't anymore. Because we are to see things in the Spirit, not in the natural sense, therefore making that saying contrary to the Word of God. To gain the testimony, you must go through the test so the season you are in now will come and it will go and then your next season will look different than it does now. You just can't give up!

*No longer will you be held hostage in a life with no repeats!*

You must change within. Outward manifestations of one's lives come from the inward exchanges of oneself. People are always changing and growing. Where you are now is not where you will always be! Do not be afraid of what is inside of you and don't be scared to be different. Some are truly crying out for help on the inside, but they never speak up for fear of being judged, so they always live bound especially by the opinions of others! They are bound by their inability to work harder to get more out of life because they have always been told that they will never be good enough or amount to anything. But even though that is the shadow of your life or mentality, that is not how you look or think in the reality of God.

In the book of Matthew, Jesus told Simon that his name was "Peter." He declared over Peter that on this rock, I will build my church and the gates of hell shall not prevail. Simon was the shadow of Peter! Never allow your past to decide your future. God's ways are not our ways, and His thoughts are not our thoughts. There is a reality to God's purpose for you that you have yet to see. But to everything there is a season, and the enemy will try to hinder your destiny, but he can't stop your destiny!

*If it were up to the enemy, you would still be a victim of abuse, but God reached down, grabbed you, and broke the yoke of slavery.*

*If it were up to the enemy, you would still be an alcoholic, but God stepped in and set you free.*

*If it were up to the enemy, you would still be an addict and a dealer, but the Holy Spirit blew on you and made you new.*

*If it were up to the enemy, you would have died in sickness and disease, but the blood of Jesus Christ Healed you!*

*If it were up to the enemy, you'd still be dancing in the clubs, but God cleaned you up, wiped you off, and made you look all brand new!*

Our God is a good God, and He is the same yesterday, today, and forevermore! It is written that God is the Author and the Finisher, the Beginning and the Ending, the Alpha and the Omega. So, what God starts in you, He is obligated to see it through! Everyone has a promise over your life but to gain more, you must give more. There must be a death in self to produce victory in Christ. The enemy thinks he has some of you right where he wants you as he did with Jesus too. He framed Jesus' crucifixion and put it on his wall but after Jesus died, he went straight to hell, grabbed the keys to hell and hades, and said, "I'm Back!" And that is exactly what you need to be telling the devil right now. Declare it now. "Devil, you can't keep me down! I'm back and I'm not going anywhere! I am going to live my reality in Christ because I no longer am the shadow of sin, but the Lord in me is now my light and my salvation!"

## POEM: THE REMNANT'S RESPONSE

On the other side of my perspective waits someone I have never met.

I think to myself, if a man can communicate without saying anything at all, then why does it take one word, one action, to cause such a great fall.

God is speaking to me; He is waiting; I just haven't arrived yet.

I know that greater is coming and that this is not the end for me, so I must change my perspective because the beginning of me must find its destiny No matter who I used to be, God has other plans for me.

But my perspective has to change, my actions forced to be rearranged all to get to one place, to see one face, because of my choice to say yes to grace.

I know that something more was on the inside of me, something new, but no one took the time to acknowledge me until God blinded me and sent me on the road to recovery.

I have learned that treasure is meant to be hidden until the keeper of it starts to open it to reveal the worth that was always within, Jesus, I am so glad I gave in.

I no longer want to be guarded and stuck in one place of mind. I must make the most of every opportunity because the days are evil, and the people are blind.

But now that You have opened my eyes to see, I have been saved, baptized, and now I'm free. I have increased in strength and confounded the wise, proving that the perspective in which I should follow was never truly mine.

CHAPTER SEVEN

# PROVOKING THE PROPHETIC

Hebrews 10:24-25 (KJV) says, "And let us consider one another to provoke unto love and to good works: not forsaking the assembly of ourselves together, as the manner of some is; but exhorting one another: and so much the more, as ye see the day approaching"

Now is the hour to draw near to God with sincere hearts and full assurance that our faith brings. The Word of God tells us to hold unswervingly to the hope that we profess, for He who promised is faithful. We have been called to provoke others towards love and good works, which requires the prophetic to arise in you, and God has chosen each one of us to speak His Word and to lift and direct one another, one prophecy and word at a time. Prophecy becomes activated with the release of another and the receiving of the person the prophecy is for.

Prophecy is the revealing of one's future through God's Word and revelation of His voice. God's Spirit, the Holy Spirit, works through a human being on earth to manifest His glory in the lives of His children.

Prophecy is also shown as an action like when Jesus was baptized by John the Baptist. See, some may not know what your prophecy is until someone else shows them who you are or what is to come in your future. Some of them didn't even know that Jesus was the Christ until afterwards. Therefore, provoking the prophetic is so vital as believers when it comes to fulfilling God's plan and purpose for our lives.

We are here to experience Heaven on earth as heirs to the Kingdom of God, which is on earth as it already is in Heaven. We are here to activate God's creation and to use what He has given us to continue producing life, which includes Spirit filled human beings that are willing to accept who they are in Christ Jesus and be used for the Master's use.

*There is a high calling, a higher calling than you could have ever imagined for yourself! Higher than the tallest mountain you have seen or the farthest star you have tried to reach.*

God calls us to have daily bread, not bread from yesterday but fresh bread, and sometimes we can get a glimpse of the bread to come even though we can't eat it yet; we know we will one day because He said it is still to come! The thing about prophecy that scares most people is that many don't want to do what is required of them to manifest their prophecy. In most cases, it requires much change and even more growth, and people are just not comfortable with that. They like to do what they want without any consequences or accountability, but in this hour, God is calling His chosen vessels to provoke the prophetic in others. God wants to take the lid off His vessels and start pouring out the contents, but there must first be an activation of release before the pouring begins.

We must understand that God provoked the prophetic in the believers living in the Old Testament days. When Jesus Christ rose from the grave in the New Testament, the New Testament believers, including you and I, would understand that God is in control of everything we do from beginning to end. He sends people into our lives to remind us of that. He is the One who allows for all things to happen and become beautiful in their own times because He created us for a specific assignment, and until that assignment is fulfilled, He will always be raising someone up who He knows will walk in obedience unto Him and meet you on your road to destiny to speak into your life and place you right where you need to be when needed. They don't always tell you the steps, but they will give you a push in the right direction.

This book has been written for someone running because of fear and He says your running days are over!

God finds you no matter where you are, and He speaks directly to your hurt, pain, fear, and shame. He speaks to your low self-esteem and mistakes, and turns those feelings and experiences into hope, trust, and strength all wrapped up in one word, Faith! Just like Elijah in I Kings 19, he ran from Jezebel in fear of her killing him, and ended up in a cave. And God asked him, "What are you doing here, Elijah?" He told God that the Israelites rejected His covenant, broke down His altars, put His prophets to death, but that he was the only one left and told God they were trying to kill him too.

Verse 11 reveals the power of God in the small things or moments. We must stop looking at prophecy as having to be BIG and Explosive or only out of the mouth of someone who yells into a microphone or dances across a stage. Prophecy does not have to be on every social media platform there is. Provoking the prophetic comes in many different ways and approaches because we are all unique and don't flow the same when releasing a word to every person. God knows how they need to be spoken to for them to receive the word! But it always takes faith to receive and to hear God's voice intentionally.

So, in this verse, God didn't come in the wind trying to speak to Elijah while He was tearing the mountains apart and shattering the rocks. God wasn't in the earthquake or the fire that came afterward. With a gentle whisper, after all the blowing of the wind, the rumbling of the earthquake, and the heat of the fire, Elijah was at his most vulnerable state. We have been at our most vulnerable state after all that has happened over the years and things to come now that we are seeing the last days come to pass.

*I believe many have been hiding because they are tired of being attacked. The wind is blowing and knocking them down. The earthquakes come and shake every foundation they have made. They are tired of fire after fire, not knowing how to put it out.*

Unfortunately, frontline soldiers get all the attacks and take all the hits first because they are called to walk through certain things, so others don't have to. This is not always fair, but that is the way it goes while God employs you.

David was employed by God and never understood why he was attacked so much by Saul. Prior to becoming King, David ended up also seeking refuge in the Cave of Adullam. All David was doing was serving Saul and he had to fight off jealousy and envy with his own leader. But even though Saul didn't honor David, David honored Saul, remained faithful, and passed up every opportunity to kill him.

David knew Kingdom principles and God says, we must remember them also. David honored ethical conduct and stayed true to his moral standards when serving his leader and God honored that.

This is a lesson learned in this hour that some will try to kill you along your prophetic journey because they see something in you that you may not even see yet. Even though that is not the kind of prophetic provoking you would like to receive, know that it is all a part of birthing the prophetic in you.

All Saul did was strengthen David for the fight, gave him strategy for the battle, and taught him patience and grace for those he would soon push to the forefront upon his departure from earth. Saul showed him what kind of leader to be and not to be. So, in my closing, whether you are the David in your story or the Saul, every choice to provoke the prophetic in others will either cause unity or division. I pray that you choose to come forth and bring unity to the Body of Christ.

Unity brings the prophetic to the forefront of your daily living! Unity adds to the building up of the saints, not the tearing down! Division will cause pieces of the puzzle to be lost but thank God He sees and knows all because every piece that has been divided will find its way back the more that we come together and do the work that God has called us to do.

*Provoking one another to good works is a command by God and in this season people of God, we are going to come out of the cave and do what thus saith the Lord!.*

CHAPTER EIGHT

# THE KINGDOM AWAKENING

Ephesians 5:14 (NIV) says, "This is why it is said: "Wake up, sleeper, rise from the dead, and Christ will shine on you."

You have been created for purpose and birthed for promise! Just like oxen laboring in a field, God has called and chosen us to labor in the Kingdom. There is a recovery process taking place on this earth to prepare us for what is to come in the supernatural. Many Christians have fallen and given up due to substance use and mental health disorders but God is a God of Restoration! According to SAMHSA, recovery is the process of change within a person who chooses to improve their health and wellness, live a self-directed life (recognizing that their attitudes, behaviors, and problems reflect their own choices not the choices of others), and striving to reach one's full potential. God has changed how we take care of ourselves by directing our focus more inwardly on getting ourselves together before using us to help others. God has told us repeatedly that He has plans and a future for us that we do not even know about yet, but He is trying to help us get there one day at a time.

**I Corinthians 2:9-10 (KJV) says, "But as it is written, Eye hath not seen, nor ear heard, nor have entered into the heart of man, the things which God has prepared for those who love him. But God hath revealed them unto us by his spirit: for the Spirit searcheth all things, yea, the deep things of God."**

Some of you have no knowledge of what your reality would be like beyond where you are right now, which is why He has put the five-fold ministry on this Earth so that the lost can be reached and the saved can be built to build! All are available to us because of Jesus Christ. The gift we never want to stop unwrapping because every time we unwrap Him, we unwrap ourselves; another part of us that we could never see, but took a Kingdom Awakening to reveal it spiritually. Everyone is unique, so finding who you are in God is the same for Scripture. God's Word never changes, but how the Word looks on and in you is different than how God's Word looks on and in someone else. Therefore, your determination mixed with the Holy Spirit leading and guiding you into all truth in God's Word is the foundation for success and recovery in this last hour for the church.

*During this Kingdom Awakening and Recovery, there are always setbacks. Still, they become setups by God for your continual growth and improvements so that internally you will be where you need to be to meet the needs of the people externally. This is called the Internal Battling for Purpose and For Promise.*

In recovery, when it comes to mental and behavioral health, we must address the trauma head on so we can move on, and that is what God is asking us to do. There is always a stigma of "what will other people think of me" but, "What will God say to you when you meet Him face to face and ask why you didn't do what He created you to do because you cared too much about what others thought? There is coming a time when God needs you whole for the assignment that He already has planned for you, but in the state that you are currently in, you wouldn't be able to sustain what He has for you at that level. So, use this time, people of God, to fix what is broken so that you can wake up from the places you have given up on because of what you have seen around you.

> *We have been created to change atmospheres, not conform to the atmosphere that people think we should live in or what others have lived in,*

So, write down health, home, purpose, and community. These four things you need to focus on in this season and get better acquainted with who you really are and what you really want out of life. When you find the answers to those questions, and you have forgiven the past and now choose to trust the future, then will be the time God will give more to you. It won't be easy, so God told me to tell His people to sustain their faith in this season! Through the ups and the downs and the challenges that will arise as you find the hidden parts of you that you didn't know existed, you must hold on to your faith and don't let go.

This past year God showed me a vision of Him holding a rope and I saw His hand reaching down to the earth for the people to climb up to get closer to Him and heaven. The people were climbing, but they couldn't hold on. They kept losing their grip! They kept giving up when it got hard! Some even let go when others were passing them by. See, we forget to give all our cares to God because He cares for us. We sit in the pews and become complacent because we don't want to put in the work to get where we want to be but then complain when what we want doesn't happen.

And while seeing this vision, I remember feeling a sense of abandonment like believers were giving up when God didn't show up when they wanted Him to while they were on this journey of climbing higher in Him. They felt frustrated, forgotten, and forsaken when really God just had other plans. Better plans! He didn't say no all the time; He was just saying not yet, but the people kept giving up.

*They kept climbing and dropping and climbing and dropping. I was wondering when someone with enough faith would be able to make it to the top of the rope.*

God says many have forgotten who you are, and you need to be awakened! You have forgotten whose you are, so you need to be awakened! And you have forgotten your assignment. I believe this is why half the members praise God and half of them don't because some are content with waiting while others have given up in their waiting. They come to be seen by others but not there to be seen and changed by God! But there is a place God is taking you in this season that you cannot afford to fall asleep in, so you must wake up and get to work.

**John 9:4 (NIV) says, "I must work the works of him that sent me, while it is day: the night cometh, when no man can work."**

God wants you to start climbing. When you think about climbing in the natural, it is difficult to climb a rope. It is a full body workout and is a great test of strength and not for the faint of heart! So, spiritually it is also a full body workout, working the mind, body, and spirit but also will be a great testing of your faith and is still not for the faint of heart but if you have faith, you will make it to the top. Even though you don't see yourself where you want to be; you must act now to have the desires of your heart later.

*It takes courage to let go of everything you have known yourself to be to trust a version of you that you cannot see, but God sees it!.*

God saw it in David. That is why He chose him for the battle! God saw it in Joseph. That is why He allowed him to live through all he did to show others that it's possible to come from the bottom but make it to the top. God saw it in Deborah, which is why He woke her up and showed her how to be the leader He created her to be! God saw it in Daniel, which is why He was able to show others what could be done when we chose to walk by faith and not by sight. The assignment on your life was put in place to destroy the yokes of bondage off of people's lives in the time and generations that God chose for you to serve so that you can help rebuild what the enemy has knocked down. The enemy has knocked down God's people but only because they have allowed him to!

*But God healed and delivered you because He has greater plans for you! God has kept you in what others have died in and offered you salvation because He has greater plans for you!*

Numbers 21:4, says that the people got discouraged because of the way. The people were not where they wanted to be even though God had already shown the Israelites that He would get them to the Promised Land. They ended up speaking against God and their leader because they gave up in their spirits and forgot what they were told to do. As a result, some of them died. You cannot speak against God and your leaders without paying a price! Their lack of true faith failed them! The rest of the Israelites still made it to the Promised Land, and I want us to be the Redeemed that makes it to Heaven and doesn't give up on God along the way.

That time has passed, and there's no getting it back now because once you're dead, you're dead. Stop wasting time, people of God, because the clock is ticking. Some now are physically dying before their time, and others we see every Wednesday and Sunday in service but have died spiritually. What happened? You stopped climbing! Not because of the Word, person, or Spirit not being present, but because you chose to stop receiving like you did at the very beginning of your journey.

God is raising up an army of people awakened in this last hour to go and speak those things that are not as though they already are. In other words, the Prophets are speaking things into existence that are already created for us and here for the taking. We just can't have it with the natural eye. We must see it already in the Spirit! But it takes our own faith and our own hands working on the part of the puzzle piece given to us to receive those things before we get to Heaven, but all things are possible to those who believe!

*So, keep climbing and never let go of the rope........*

CHAPTER NINE

# THE RENEWAL OF THE WATCHMAN

Isaiah 56:10-11 (NIV) says, "Israel's watchmen are blind, they all lack knowledge; they are all mute dogs, they cannot bark; they lie around and dream, they love to sleep. They are dogs with mighty appetites; they never have enough. They are shepherds who lack understanding; they all turn to their own way, they seek their own gain."

God is renewing us to the true knowledge of His image, but here is where the problem is in the church. The watchmen that are meant to warn us of danger are like dumb dogs who don't watch. When danger comes, they are sleeping instead of warning! The people have lost focus on the watchman's assignment, and they have fallen asleep. We are called to reach lost souls, help protect them, and then build them up. When the watchman does not watch, pray, and discern, the people will die if they are not prepared when calamity comes.

Many people were given a word when it was calm and weren't under attack in many different directions, but where are they now? Now that true prophecy is being fulfilled?! Were they then false prophets?

Yes, not everyone who claims to be a prophet and gives you "a word from the Lord," is truly in a relationship with Christ and the Holy Spirit. This leads me to now understand and see why they caused hell during the good times and sat down when times got hard. Then some believers would rather sit on the lies of the enemy than speak up, standing on the promises of God, to lead God's people during a crisis. Some are guilty of becoming lazy and now bound to what feels good instead of what's right. Losing sight of the cause and now it has affected us all in some way, shape, or form. Every door has been attacked and every sleeping warrior has been unaccounted for!

I believe many people today are gnawing away at life like a dog chewing on a bone, craving and needing more but still always lacking but that hunger must be for something permanent, not temporary. That bone will not last, but the blood will. The blood of Jesus Christ washes, cleanses, frees, covers, and empowers us. We must submerge ourselves in God in this season like a submarine goes under the water and doesn't come up until the task is finished. Our perspective must go deeper, and our territory must be enlarged.

We must stop exploiting that mentality of being a Christian but thinking it's okay to still act like the world. We are not meant to do what everybody else is doing. Not if we want to go to a place in God that we have never been. We are to resemble Christ, but we have been seeing more of the resemblance of wolves in sheep's clothing. Why? First, they are trespassing on private territory because anyone who operates in the Kingdom of God will not go unseen, and many are operating illegally, meaning not in the position that God created them for. Secondly, they have lost their covering, therefore trying to fit into something they were never meant to wear or operate in.

During this shaking, many have realized that where they are is not where they were meant to be. This happens when people just go start ministries on their own without any covering or protection! This happens when those in authority give authority to others who are not ready to have authority but think they are! Then when they get to a place of getting tired of working without having God's hand in what they are doing, they are now upset and angry. They are transferring their frustrations to others instead of just admitting that they missed the mark, which would allow God to move them forward instead of feeling stuck and weighed down and in the wrong place. Many need to sit down, serve, and find who they truly are in God, but a lack of covering has kept them going and we are seeing the bleeding drip down. **All the Watchmen that we have in place are not the Watchmen that are keeping us safe! But that is going to change.**

*So, We must be assertive and careful in this season. This is not a time to play patty cake with your neighbor! This is a time to get right, repent, and return to your position in God!*

Destruction of this world is coming, but this is still the greatest hour of the church. Revelation has already been provided, but here is another problem that we must fix. If we already know God raises some up and sits some down, then why are so many believers arguing about politics instead of just praying for our leaders? Whether we agree with them or not! As Christians, we are chosen to dig in the dark places and find the treasure that has been hidden. Each person has been chosen to discover a certain piece of the puzzle, but the puzzle will not be complete until you do. So, these watchmen are supposed to be watching for the enemy before he gets to our territory. Even if we don't think they are qualified for those positions, we must still respect and honor them through God. God puts up and takes down, so if it's going to be done, then He will use someone to make the necessary changes. Until then, pray for your leaders!

I think of the Watchman as being the four corners of the puzzle! Not every piece will fit instantly in the location you are trying to complete, but every corner piece will be shaped to perfection. The renewal has already started to take place and new watchmen are arising, and each one of you have a set and prepared time.

God is lighting the way and bringing structure and order back into the Body of Christ through His Word but are we listening? The reason why watchmen get distracted is because they stop hearing God! How do you distinguish God's voice from Satan's? Well, the Bible says, "My sheep know my voice and a stranger they will not follow." This means that if I'm of God I will follow his voice and not the enemies.

> *If your actions are causing division instead of unity, then you know the voice that you are hearing is not the voice of God. If the words you speak are contrary to the Word of God, then you are not hearing the voice of God. Does what you do line up with the Word or contradict it? Does it promote conviction or manifest condemnation? Does your life market God or do you send others down the road of destruction?*

It is important to know that God has allowed what has happened to happen in our lives and nothing gets past God! If you are the watchman that has not done a very good job watching God's people, then now is the time to change, and He knew it would be now for you. He knows what is coming before we do, so the moment you decide to ask for a second chance, taking full responsibility for your actions, He is already there waiting for you. The Remnants are Rising with the flow and order of God. Where there is no order, there is chaos and confusion. God is not the author of confusion. So, God reveals things to His prophets so that they can speak and warn the people ahead of time so that people's lives don't get wasted, but not everyone listens and responds quickly.

**Amos 3:7 (NIV) says, "Surely the Sovereign Lord does nothing without revealing his plan to his servants the prophets."**

But instead of hearing God and being obedient, many are using what's going on around them as tools to divide, manipulate, and weaken other people giving fuel to the enemy when we are meant to fight the enemy together; he just keeps getting away with pulling us apart.

> *Our focus should not be in Washington, but it should be within! God is breaking tradition! Systems and barriers are being broken! Walls are coming down!*

Like the sound of a train coming, it gives a signal so that you can hear it in time to be ready. A train is heard even before getting to your area. God is sounding the alarm! Joel 2:1 says (NIV), "Blow the trumpet in Zion, sound the alarm on my holy hill. Let all who live in the land tremble, for the day of the Lord is coming! It is close at hand." Some have gotten lost in the land of Assyria and driven to Egypt because they have lost focus on God, but He is calling us back to him! A great trumpet is being blown and we will be brought to our knees.

There must be a renewal of the watchman. In Ezekiel 33:1-6 (NIV) which says, "Again the word of the Lord came unto me saying, Son of man, speak to the children of they people, and say unto them, When I bring the sword upon a land, if the people of the land take a man of their coasts, and set him for their watchman: If then he seeth the sword come upon the land, he blow the trumpet, and warn the people; Then whosoever heareth the sound of the trumpet, and taketh not warning; if the sword come, and take him away, his blood shall be upon his own head. He heard the sound of the trumpet, and took not warning; his blood shall be upon him. But he that taketh warning shall deliver his soul. **But if the watchman see the sword come, and blow not the trumpet, and the people be not warned; if the sword come, and take any person from among them, he is taken away in his iniquity; but his blood will I require at the watchman's hand.**"

*Our job as leaders is to warn the people and prepare them for what's to come before it gets here. No one was prepared for Covid-19, but we had a sense of something that was coming. We read in Revelations 5 of what is to come. People are afraid to talk about it but not the true prophets! Not the true Watchman of the Last Days. We must discuss the white horse and how it represents the antichrist that will deceive many. Speaking peace but waging war! We must discuss the red horse and how it represents wars that will break out and kill many "shedding innocent blood." We must discuss the black horse and how it represents the famine in the land, and how the pale horse represents death and a wiping out of 1/4 of the Earth with famines, plagues and we are seeing that in these last times being fulfilled right before our eyes.*

I am grieved by those who want to complain about what's happening, but not willing to put the work in to change it! If you don't stand up for something, you will fall for everything! Listen, we do not receive grace for the things we do or the stuff we acquire. It is only by the love, grace, and mercy of God. This generation must understand the importance of knowing their assignment and its responsibility of it because you do not want to be called a watchman by God and get blood on your hands for not doing the right things by His chosen people.

*You may love the title, but the responsibility of it is far greater than you, and that must continue to be at the forefront of your reason for submitting to the assigned mission as watchman of the Kingdom of God!*

CHAPTER TEN

# THE BREAKING OF FERTILE GROUND

Hosea 10:12 (NIV) says, "Sow righteousness for yourselves, reap the fruit of unfailing love, and break up your unplowed ground; for it is time to seek the Lord, until he comes and showers his righteousness on you."

This is a season the fervent prayers of the righteous are coming alive! We have interceded regarding the challenges that we have had to face and it has caused us to drop to our knees and ask God when it will be over? But Jesus says in John 12:24 (NIV), "Very truly I tell you, unless a kernel of wheat falls to the ground and dies, it remains only a single seed. But if it dies, it produces many seeds." So even though we have had many recent trials and tribulations, we remained faithful and intact with God. Now, Jesus is saying it's not about us, but it is up to us! He is telling you that life always springs from death which is why this is the greatest hour for the church! You, being that one kernel, and going through all you have, produced many seeds, and now is The Breaking of Fertile Ground.

A farmer in the natural must do all the work above ground before the seed underground starts to grow, but in the Spirit, the seed must start growing within to start producing outwardly. Beloved, we are birthed out of darkness! Go back to when you were in your mother's womb. A child inside the womb lives in darkness and solitude for nine months before being born. I wonder, did we grow to full capacity while we were in our mother's womb or do we grow in fullness after birth until our death? If you think about it, a seed already has everything in it that it will become. So as a baby grows, we are like a seed who already has everything within us that we will become, everything that makes us who we are, and then after we are born, the body just automatically does what it's supposed to. We get taller, our legs get longer, and our hair grows. Then after many years, it is already in us, for our hair to turn grey, for wrinkles to start to appear, our bodies get weaker, and our mind is not as sharp. We become like children needing to be taken care of, but we all started as a baby in a womb. A seed in darkness!

A seed must be placed inside of darkness and beneath the ground before it starts to grow. The transformation has been proven to begin even inside the tomb when Jesus died, was buried, but then rose on the third day. There must be a period of darkness before the light can make itself known. What about Heaven? Heaven was created by God and is real to the believer only by belief within oneself. Without belief, there is darkness, but with belief, the truth can then reside. This season is fertile ground for the believer!

> *The entrance of God's Words gives light to what is already yours. That is why the enemy doesn't want you producing because he is after your seed. The enemy tried to kill and bury you but really, he planted you and now the very soil that he used to try to kill you, you are using to produce others like you!*

You are the seed of Abraham! This is your growing season. The ground is fertile, and your harvest is coming! We need to understand that to grow, you must know what God wants from you during this time in your life. You must allow yourself to be watered and nourished by the right things but to receive, you must give up something. Give up old mindsets, toxic relationships, habits of co-dependency and inconsistencies to receive new visions and ideas, so that you may walk into divine connections and see new faces. Embrace success in building your life with the blocks God is putting in your hands. This is a time when God is giving you a picture and what He wants, blocks being in your hands, and now He is saying build the picture I have given you but do it my way only! No revisions! No what if's! No, I think it'll work this way or that way! Build only the picture that He has already made for you.

Spiritually, that is where this world has gotten it wrong. Now the harvest of some fruit that has been planted and sown is coming up, no one knows what to do. Now, people are asking God to give them relief when they didn't listen in the first place to where He wanted them to be planted nor where the sowing should have been.

*The good news is that growing up takes some falling down, but for every fall we get another strategy on what it takes to Rise Again!*

Failing to allow your seed to do its created purpose is more devastating than death! When you think of a graveyard, death automatically comes to mind. So, I want you to picture yourself being born with dreams, visions, and purpose but then you die and everything in you never had the opportunity to manifest. You're no longer here and everything inside you is forced to be buried. Sadly, you departed this life not completing everything you were supposed to do while on this earth. I call this the graveyard perspective. You do not want to go back in the ground still full of seed because here's the thing: when you are born with the seed, it becomes alive and active in you, but when you die, that seed dies with you. The Bible tells us that a stillborn child is better off than the man that lives but never fulfills his purpose. Do you choose temporary pain and darkness that will produce growth for your breakthrough, or will you stay where you are and when the time comes for harvest, you will not have the capacity to hold what comes up? Fertile ground causes you to let go of the environment you are used to and pushes and elevates you to a place you have never been. God is reconstructing some things on the inside so that when you see the construction on the outside, you will know how to handle it! When you can carry the fruit of the Spirit and allow the process to take place, your harvest is going to be love, joy, peace, forbearance, kindness, goodness, faithfulness, gentleness, and self-control. There will always be seedtime and harvest.

**Genesis 8:22 (NIV) says, "As long as the earth endures, seedtime and harvest, cold and heat, summer and winter, day and night will never cease."**

So, what you allow to influence you, you will reap from, good or bad. You don't want to reap dead fruit in a season that was meant to change your life for the better and launch you into your next. Now you missed your season of prosperity because of procrastination and a lack of discipline.

While operating in the prophetic, we are the bridge that connects the person to their future in God. Therefore we must be a strong bridge that others can cross to have a better chance of surviving the storms that will come to try to kill their harvest. But you have to tell Satan that he can't have your seed now or never! God already prepared a way for you in the Spirit. All you must do is find it! You are the incorruptible seed that is due for breakthrough. When we have an expectation, God will always surrender a manifestation and multiplication of fruit. We are about to see the birthing of Heaven on earth like never before. There have been labor pains in the Spirit and now the ground is breaking, and the seed is about to see the light of day, and when it does, it's going to start growing and producing quickly! So be ready!

Put your ear to the ground and respond to the sound quickly. There is a breaking of fertile ground and the shift has come. God's Word living in us is what produces life through us. There is power in your words and words produce life. So live and not die and declare the works of our Lord! Always remember that one plants, another waters, but God brings the increase. So, in Him, your value will always go up!

CHAPTER ELEVEN

# THE PLAYGROUND OF CHRISTIANITY

James 4:7 (NIV) says, "Submit yourselves therefore to God. Resist the devil, and he will flee from you."

This has been a time of Spiritual Warfare for the Body of Christ. Yet, it has been a needed season of reconstruction and resubmission to God. There have been too many fallen soldiers on the battlefield because of the attacks that stem from their mistakes. In times of crisis, I have seen the strength of good leadership by how they respond. We are built to last, especially in hard times, but where we mess up at is letting down our shield and allowing ourselves to be hit and hurt by the enemy not by action but just by manipulation of the mind.

James 4:7 is easy to read but sure is hard to follow when you are used to operating in your flesh and not handling the cares of this world spiritually. Satan likes to play baseball and he loves to be the pitcher…in control! So, in this life, God calls our name daily because it's our turn to step up to the plate. Now, God allows the enemy to throw the pitch, but He also has given us the tools and teaching to know when and how to swing. First, the enemy throws an outside pitch, so he messes with things outside your reach to distract you from hitting the ball. Then he throws an inside pitch to hurt us deeply, to use the people closest to us to keep us from hitting the ball. But then he throws the curve ball. This pitch is the one that tries to take you out of the game, but God has requested a breakthrough in your life and at this very moment, your actions to what is going on around you are going to change.

As Christians, this is not a game of competition on a playground. This is about striving to become all that we are meant to be and to believe God's Word and always submit to Him so that we resist the tactics of the enemy and by doing this, we will get on base every single time. We are to encourage all hitters to get on base because this is not a fight between the flesh, but we war in the Spirit. There are too many in competition with one another. God is fed up with seeing His people operating in a space at less capacity because they are too worried about someone else, which has stung their own growth.

This is a heart issue, and the enemy will take that issue and throw you pitches and strike you out all day, until you get it right with others and you get it right with God. Listen, we have already come too far to act petty like a child who wants to swing at the swing set, but all the swings are taken, so they throw a fit standing there watching the other kids swing instead of enjoying something else they like to do until the next swing comes available. Too many people are looking at other people's plates and while looking and admiring other plates, theirs is getting cold and after a while it becomes too cold to eat so then you throw it away. Throwing away purpose because you don't know who you are and don't understand the timing of God. Reheating food in the microwave is not the same when it is first prepared and hot. It's not the same as fresh manna. Can you say, "Amen!"

The Bible tells us that out of the heart flows the issues of life. So where is our heart and is it really in the game? When we love God, we will submit to Him and allow the Holy Spirit to lead us from the beginning to the end of the game while encouraging our teammates so that we can all partake in what God wants to do while we are here. One person cannot play the game alone! One person cannot score all the runs! We have already been given the power to hit the ball and place it where it needs to go, but we tend to forget who we are and what our purpose is as children of God and our purpose on this team. Everyone has different positions and different responsibilities. We must stop allowing the enemy to hinder our access to the storehouses of our blessings in the Kingdom of God. You can be competitive in a healthy way, but when it starts hindering another person or you, there is a problem that must be addressed.

*Every decision and choice you make has a purpose and it's based on principles that you follow which produces what you believe!*

If we are not producing in the Kingdom, we will not receive the promises from the Kingdom. So, if you choose not to play in the game as a team player, you will not receive the reward of being a winner of the game. Satan assigns demons to this game to take you out! But the devil is a liar! You must get up to bat every day and tell the devil that he is not taking you out! That you are not quitting! No matter what you have to face, you know that God is with you!

*I pray that every weary soul is awakened and get back in the game. I speak to every dry place in your life to start flowing again and may you want and need to play the game be restored in the name of Jesus. I speak to every sleepy player that has not had rest to rest in the Lord beloved, and you will be awakened again and receive strength and encouragement to pick you back up and be what the team needs to make it to the last inning in Jesus name. Amen!*

I think of a globe and it's like some people feel like they are inside of it. Watching the days go by and the kingdom expanding but feel like they are not a part of it! God has you here right now to tell you that you are a part of it but moving forward, that is all up to you on if you will choose to lay down your life and follow Him. We have been given power and authority to overcome everything that tries to strike us out of the game! Authority is our position in Christ. We know that whatever we ask for and speak, we can have if we believe. Power is the power of God working through us by the Holy Spirit. In one day in prayer, I saw a vision of children playing on a playground, but this wasn't a typical playground. Usually, children who want to swing will be by the swings and the children who want to slide will be at the slide. They are happy and in position for what they need and where they want to be.

But in this vision, the children were out of place! They are not in a place where they want to be, know they should be, and not in the place God has designed them to be. This is The Playground of Christianity, my brothers and sisters! Christianity is the religion of the person and the teachings of Jesus Christ, the name above every name. Many believers in the Body of Christ believe in God and Jesus, know who He is, have heard the Word preached, read the Word, and still refuse to live in who the Word says they are because they have chosen to be complacent because of fear of the unknown! It is good to get out of comfort zones and try new things, but some people get stuck and remain in a place they were only meant to be temporary, like that little girl earlier waiting for the swing. She could leave temporarily but after a moment, she must return to her assigned place! There are believers still sitting on the bench that need to get out and play!

*There are still believers that need to be sliding down the slide, but they are still sitting ducks, unhappy and allowing the enemy to hold them hostage, swinging on a swing but going nowhere! I ask you, where are you in this vision?*

Job lost everything, but he received double because he accepted change and went with it. He was trusting God the entire time. David had to look fear in the face and take on the giant trying to kill him. David had to rise up and take courage and heart for the shifting in his life. Daniel was stuck in the lion's den, but he showed up for the war with his flesh, but acted in the Spirit and that took faith to believe because he had to live. Where he was; was not where he would always be! Esther was purposely isolated for a season, and I know that gets lonely sometimes and you feel misunderstood in the church and by those closest to you. Still, she obeyed wisdom submitted, and ended up saving her family and all those connected to her. Understand that our flesh is subject to what we say and do in the Spirit. So, we must stop forgetting our authority in the Kingdom!

Without God's presence, there is no freedom, so without Him walking with you on the playground, you are going to get lost in transition every time. His thoughts of you are higher than the thoughts you have for yourself. The plans you have, God says He has bigger!

**Proverbs 19:21 (NIV) says, "Many are the plans in a man's heart, but it is the Lord's purpose that will prevail."**

Moving forward, it's important to talk about the birthing of our assignment in Christ. We cannot have another person's baby! We cannot birth another person's assignment! We cannot operate in another person's anointing! The oil drips, but everyone still has their own way of doing things and God made it like that for a reason. These words are going to turn a light on in you and illuminate the way you see God and understand his Word in this season of your life. We are to carry and prepare what He has given us to birth and manifest what He wants to see out of us to produce after our kind.

> *He keeps the production going! He knows that some employees won't show up, some will quit, some may only work part time, so He assigns us all for something so that when one person doesn't show up, the work can still go on! So, in moving forward to hold the promise of a thing, we must first be prepared to birth it!*

When you operate in your position in the Kingdom, you must spend time with the one who has the job description! It's not enough to walk around playing and calling yourself a Christian but losing every battle that you're faced with! God cannot heal what we choose not to confront. He can't use us if we refuse to move out of the place we are in and the mindset that we've had in our toxic space. We can't climb up the mountain of freedom still being tied to the valley of tradition.

## DECREE & DECLARE

**Every spirit of anxiety** that comes to worry you and causes emotional and physical impairment, Holy Spirit, move on every person that is reading this now. We bind up the spirit of anxiety and release the blood of Jesus. Anxiety has been left on the cross and you are letting anxiety go right now in the name of Jesus. Amen.

**Every spirit of fear and intimidation** comes to paralyze Christians, so God's work will cease through you, but Holy Spirit move on every person reading this and by faith, we bind up the spirit of fear and intimidation and release the blood of Jesus Christ. You are defeated fear and intimidation and you have no room in the mind of God's people in the name of Jesus. Amen.

**Every spirit of rejection** that comes to make you forget who you are and whose you are, Holy Spirit, move on every person reading this and you are accepted into the beloved. The blood of Jesus sealed your future. You are walking into a new identity in Christ. Amen.

**Every spirit of depression and oppression** that wants you to call it quits that wants you to shut your mouth, Holy Spirit, move on every person reading this. We bind up the spirit of depression and oppression, it must leave right now in the name of Jesus. You are more than a conqueror in Jesus' name. Amen.

**Every spirit of suicide** that says just give in, just give up, just take your life because no one will care if your gone, I bind you in the name of Jesus and loose forth the Holy Spirit. The Spirit that tells you that you are going to live and not die and declare the works of the Lord. The Spirit that says that there is nothing that you can't overcome with Jesus Christ and there is nothing that you have done that could keep God from loving you right where you are in Jesus' name. Amen.

**Every spirit of doubt** that wants you to question everything and cause confusion in your life we bind right now in the name of Jesus. Holy Spirit move on every person reading this. God's promises are yes and amen and they choose to seek first the Kingdom of God and all His righteousness and everything they need will be added to them in Jesus' name. Amen.

CHAPTER TWELVE

# TAKE THE BAND-AID OFF

**J**eremiah 30:17 (NIV) says, "But I will restore you to health and heal your wounds , declares the Lord, because you are called outcast, Zion for whom no one cares."

This chapter may hurt a bit when it's all said and done, but God will step in and fix what is broken and heal what is hurt. The Word of God is alive and active, working through all those who choose to believe, receive, and step into their assignments as children of God no matter what yesterday said about you or done to you. We must never forget that Jesus Christ died for us and rose on the third day so that we could live free, live whole, and so that we could be different, and our lives could be better!

**John 10:10 (NIV) says, "The thief comes only to steal, kill, and destroy; I have come that they may have life, and have it to the full."**

Light already conquered darkness and goodness conquered sin. Nothing can hold you down when you call on the name of the Lord unless you allow it to. It may look like it's impossible or that it will never change, but all things are possible with God. He is the almighty God! Our God split the Red Sea, caused dead bodies to rise, sick bodies to instantly be healed, and blind eyes to open. He is everywhere all the time, showing His Glory through every believer that chooses to not give up but speak up and ask for help. Everything in God is also in you, but you must find it and use it because faith without works is dead.

*You cannot just have faith and sit down. Faith causes movement and momentum!*

God gave me a vision of the Earth one early morning as soon as I woke up. I saw the earth with a band-aid on it and God removed the band-aid from the Earth to allow the infection to be exposed so that it could be cleaned, healed, and back to working at full capacity! God showed me what was happening in the natural, but He was really about to operate in the supernatural.

We have been hurting as a nation! We have been hurting as people! We have been operating and living in rebellion, but God wants to change that and reposition, rebuild, and reconstruct us because He has a whole new focal point for our eyes to zone in on. This is why we must get in alignment with what He is doing.

He had pulled the band-aid off, allowing us to go through this pandemic like birthing pains and growing pains through the process of change. So, what has happened is that people have operated more in the flesh and the enemy thinks he has won. He took something that happened and created chaos, but it's only chaotic to those who choose to see the world in the natural because it has already been taken care of in the Spirit. Many are just not seeing it that way, but God can change that in you if you allow Him to. We have been given grace to still operate how we need to during this time of transition. It doesn't have to be chaotic for us as believers.

The Christ in you matters to him! The enemy wants power and control over you.

*You don't matter to the enemy; Jesus Christ in you matters to the enemy.*

So, he will do everything he can during the little time he has left to try to stop you, but now is the time to start learning your opponent. Most study up on him but some of you have never listened to a teaching on who the devil is and his tactics. It is a must if you are a Christian! It's not enough to have Christ but you must know how to recognize when you have allowed Christ to leave and the enemy to come in. God must be number one in your life every moment of every day. When you have Him as number one, you will know how to deal with the enemy moving forward when he shows up.

*For so long, He has not been number one in the lives of many believers, but He is a nail fastened in a sure place. And the same nails that He hung on and went through Jesus are the same nails that hold you and I together.*

Jesus Christ has come to heal the broken hearted and bind up their wounds. I believe that is why He was showing me the earth with a band-aid on it and then Him taking it off because there is much mending that needs to be done and intercession that needs to take place. When you take the letters in earth and rearrange them, it spells "heart." So the heart of Christ is His people and right now the hearts of the earth are wounded. But God wants to change that and to change you so that your wounds will heal. The wounds of the land cannot continue to hurt and bleed out. God must heal these places in you so that He can reveal the healing virtue of himself from you. Things happen spiritually and then manifest themselves naturally. That is what has caused this, a rebellious nation.

People of God have gotten weak and have quit pursuing purpose and producing the fruit of the Spirit. But the Bible says, "weeping may endure for a day, but joy cometh in the morning."

Right now, people of God, we must acknowledge that we have messed up! The spirit of racism runs rapid. The spirit of offense hasn't left, but his stay is long overdue. The world is taking what's good and mocking it then conforming it to fit their own beliefs and twisted pleasures. There's still too much injustice in the land and we must heal so that we can speak up on these issues and make a difference where we can.

*No one can make a positive change if they are bleeding out poisonous toxins.*

We must stop being silent! We always say if we want to see the change, we must be the change. This is not just a quote that sounds good, but it's something we must eat, chew, and swallow. **Every member of the body has been affected and infected by this.** No one among us is perfect. We all fall short and need someone to help us pray and fast to see the change we need to make for the healing to occur. Everything from entertainment to sports stopped, the economy was questionable for a moment, unemployment was at its highest, stock markets crashed, thousands of deaths, idolatry popping up everywhere and showing its wicked face. The love for money and power raised the bar, and public calamity on a nation that caused great and sudden damage and distress and disaster, but God has started healing us again.

You see, the Earth is wounded and it's trying to cover up itself with the things of this world because that is what the people have allowed to consume them. People try to cover themselves up, so no one sees the wounds, but God said no more.

> *People have put food before God. Eating out is not bad, but we have become consumed with fast food that we have been missing fellowship in our households with our families. We have put sports before God. Watching sports is fine, but not when it takes you out of the game as the player on God's Team or when it takes you away from assembling at your church; not when it takes you out of relationship with the Father. We have put money before God. Having money is not the problem, but the love of money is! We have put our lives before God. Taking care of ourselves is a must but when was the last time we asked God if He liked how we are living? We have put the government before God. Following laws of the land is a must but I ask you whose report are you really believing? The government rests on the shoulders of Jesus Christ and God places Him as the head. What this world has done is try to work its way to the top and take God out of everything. We have put worldly education before God. So, schools were closed. Education is needed but the knowledge of and the revelation of God's Word must be taught to our children.*

But even though those things were taken away, now we see ourselves getting some things back and in better shape.

> *It's like when someone finds and takes care of you then sends you on your way again. Now you are different because it's not just the healing that took place on you but the healing that took place in you!*

In Luke, the Good Samaritan used oil and wine for the man's wounds. On earth the band-aid needs to be taken off to allow Jesus to come and heal us. Jesus was anointed prior to His death. The lady with the Alabaster box broke it, poured the oil over Jesus' head before his crucifixion. And then Mary wiped His feet with her hair and washed His feet with her tears.

So, the blood of Jesus Christ is the ointment that will heal the wounds that we have, individually and as a whole nation. God is breaking tradition, and everything is changing from here.

**Proverbs 20:30 (NIV) says, "Blows and wounds scrub away evil, and beatings purge the inmost being."**

God is forming an alignment and preparation for the coming of Jesus Christ. So, now we must take the correction and this beating that we have been through, and we must repent. Jesus will not come until all have had the chance to hear the gospel, so we want to be ready in hopes that all are saved.

*Fulfilling the will of God requires repentance.*

**II Chronicles 7:14 (NIV) says, "If my people, who are called by my name, will humble themselves and pray and seek my face and turn from their wicked ways, then I will hear from heaven, and I will forgive their sin and will heal their land."**

Brothers and Sisters, He will heal our land! We are still getting our land that flows with milk and honey, but we must surrender first and admit our wrongs so that He can make the wrong right again. Please notice that honey symbolizes health, and the stripes of Jesus Christ already heal us, so health is already ours! Milk symbolizes eternal life, fertility, and abundance and we know, prophecy tells us, that more is coming!

Now, it is up to us to get in position with God the Father. We are a generation that will Rise from this and do even greater works by the coming of Christ. God is revealing the gates of repentance to us, showing us how we should walk in the way of peace and truth under a sovereign God, no longer covering things up but revealing them so the healing can begin.

We must take back what the enemy stole from us! We have been given power and authority over this land through the operation of The Holy Spirit. We will stand up for what we believe in and that is the healing power of God. We have gone from grieving to healing and even though we have not gone this way before, God will be with us every step of the way, but you must take the band-aid off and let Him take care of you.

*We have been given this chance to make it right with God so let's take it and move on.*

I am excited about the future, and I know that you will do great things for the Kingdom! Don't give up and fall into temptation. Put on your whole armor, get up, and go to work. Don't live in fear because God has not given us the spirit of fear but of power, love, and a sound mind. One day I looked at the world from only one view, but then one day my viewpoint changed. Now, it's not about what I see in my present. It's about what I don't see that holds my future and yours also. God Bless You and Keep You in Jesus' name, Amen!

# ABOUT THE AUTHOR

Evangelist Amber Brown is a Spiritual Motivator and sought-after Revivalist out of Poplar Bluff Missouri, as well as the Radio Host for Rise To The Mission Radio Show through Awakening Prophetic Radio Network USA/World. Rise to The Mission International, started in 2017 after writing her first book as she started traveling and ministering God's Word. Amber is the Author of Rise To The Mission and Co-Author of Shaking Hands With Wisdom. She attends The International College of Bible Theology where she is pursuing her education in Theology and Christian Counseling. She holds many certifications in the mental health/behavioral health field as well as stays extensively involved in public relations and community networking within her community and surrounding areas. Amber's mission is to reach the lost and lead them to the gates of Salvation through Jesus Christ, and to encourage the Body of Christ and build them up for battle in these last days. She equips you for the work of service and servanthood while charging you and challenging you to grasp your identity in fulfilling your mission given to you before the very foundations of the world. She is a mother of two beautiful children and stays active on assignment in the Kingdom.

Amber is a Certified Peer Specialist as well as a Missouri Associate Alcohol and Drug Counselor I with certificates in Wellness and Recovery and Mental Health First Aid and is currently working on her MAADC II Certificate. Amber is also an active member in her communities Crisis Intervention and Suicide Prevention teams as well as the Community Advisory Board. Amber works full time with a local non-profit Certified Community Behavioral Health Organization, assisting and serving individuals in the community and surrounding counties.

She is an active member at Mt. Calvary Powerhouse Church in Poplar Bluff, MO, where she serves as a Licensed Minister and Sunday School teacher in the children's ministry as well as the church, under the guidance and leadership of Bishop Ron Webb and First Lady Dr. Georgia Webb.

Amber speaks at seminars, conferences, youth groups, schools, revivals, and recovery groups all over the United States and soon to be internationally. She speaks to individuals of all ages on how to apply their faith to the realities of life. She encourages individuals by sharing her story of overcoming sin and difficulty by the power of her maturing relationship with God, to rise and reach their full potential in all areas of their lives.

Amber enjoys being outdoors and spending time with her family. She loves to participate in community events to help build unity within the community. She believes that to reach the world effectively you must start in your own community first! Amber is consistently continuing her education and schooling to continue her growth as an individual and a daughter of Christ. She looks forward to achieving and reaching her goal of a doctoral with hard work and dedication.

Amber believes in building up others and inspiring them to grasp their identities within their community, while encouraging them to live their life abundantly in His power and grace. On this foundation of belief, two years ago Amber started her "Rise to the Mission" interview shows. These shows focus on learning the missions of individuals. Allowing them to share their stories on how they overcame adversity, trials, and tribulations. These individuals share the steps they took to "Rise to the Mission" and provide resources and encouragement to others.

If you would like to contact Amber for speaking engagements or book ordering, email her at risetothemission@gmail.com or visit her website at www.amberbrownministries.com.

# INDEX

## A

abandonment, 49
Abraham, 16, 61
abundance, 76
accountability, 16, 25, 43
Action of Alteration, 23, 25
activation, 20, 43
addict, 18, 40
addiction, 6
adjustments, 26
adversary, 29
adversity, 2, 34, 80
afraid, 33, 39, 58
airplane, 27
Alabaster box, 75
alarm, 27, 57
alcoholic, 40
alignment, 72, 76
alpha, 40
altar, 24, 27
alterations, 24, 26
Ambassadors, 32
Amber Brown, 78

analogy, 10
angry, 55
anointing, 2, 68
antichrist, 58
anxiety, 69
Arise, 11
army, 4, 52
asleep, 50, 53
assertive, 55
assignment, 9, 15, 20, 44, 48, 50, 51, 53, 58, 68, 78
atmosphere, 31, 49
atmospheres, 49
attack, 11, 41, 53
attitudes, 47
author, 40, 56
authority, 5, 34, 37, 38, 40, 54, 55, 67, 68, 77
Authority, 67
Awakening, 47, 48, 78

B

baby, 60, 68
band-aid, 72, 73, 75, 77
baptized, 41, 43
barriers, 38, 57
baseball, 64
battle, 4, 21, 46, 51, 69, 78
beautiful, 11, 44, 78
beginning, 15, 18, 36, 40, 41, 44, 52, 66
behaviors, 47
believe, 1, 9, 15, 19, 23, 31, 34, 45, 50, 52, 54, 65, 66, 67, 68, 71, 73, 77
believer, 2, 60, 72

believers, 4, 6, 9, 25, 43, 49, 54, 55, 67, 68, 73
bench, 67
benefits, 37
Bible, 3, 8, 13, 15, 56, 62, 66, 74, 78
bills, 18
birth, 13, 14, 16, 29, 60, 68, 69
birthed, 11, 35, 47, 60
Bishop Ron Webb, 79
black horse, 58
blind, 41, 53, 72
blood, 10, 40, 54, 57, 58, 69, 70, 76
bold, 2, 10, 34
bondage, 51
book, 6, 14, 20, 26, 39, 44, 78, 80
bread, 9, 17, 43
breakthrough, 14, 23, 62, 65
breath of resurrection, 9
brick wall, 33
brokenness, 24
brothers, 27, 38, 67
building, 4, 5, 24, 25, 46, 61, 80
buried, 3, 60, 61
business, 6, 7, 20
butterflies, 17

C

calamity, 31, 53, 74
Call to Action, 6
car, 31
Cave of Adullam, 45
Certified Peer Specialist, 79
challenges, 6, 49, 59

chaos, 27, 34, 56, 72
children, 9, 18, 36, 42, 57, 60, 66, 67, 71, 75, 78, 79
choice, 8, 18, 26, 41, 46, 66
choices, 10, 37, 47
Christ, 1, 3, 7, 8, 9, 10, 12, 13, 14, 15, 19, 29, 32, 38, 40, 43, 46, 47, 48, 54, 56, 64, 67, 68, 69, 70, 71, 73, 75, 76, 77, 78, 79
Christian, 14, 69, 73, 78
Christianity, 29, 64, 67
church, 2, 3, 5, 6, 7, 9, 11, 13, 19, 20, 24, 25, 30, 33, 38, 39, 48, 53, 55, 59, 68, 75, 79
citizens, 19
climbing, 49, 50, 51, 52
club, 40
co-dependency, 61
cold, 62, 65
comfort, 37, 38, 67
comfortable, 1, 3, 7, 10, 37, 43
commitment, 32
communion, 31
communities, 19, 79
community, 30, 49, 78, 79, 80
competition, 65
complacent, 3, 9, 27, 29, 37, 49, 67
compromise, 9
condemnation, 56
conferences, 79
confirm, 30
confront, 19, 69
confusion, 56, 70
conquered, 1, 71
construction, 62
conviction, 56
counsel, 33, 34

courage, 50, 68
Covid-19, 9, 58
COVID-19, 18
creation, 3, 31, 43
crisis, 54, 64
cross, 62, 69
crucifixion, 40, 76

D

danger, 53
darkness, 8, 20, 24, 25, 38, 60, 62, 71
David, 9, 45, 46, 51, 68
day, 4, 6, 7, 8, 9, 10, 23, 31, 42, 43, 47, 50, 57, 60, 62, 63, 65, 66, 67, 71, 73, 74, 77
dead, 8, 47, 51, 62, 72
death, 10, 13, 38, 40, 44, 58, 59, 60, 61, 75
Deborah, 51
deceive, 58
deception, 16
decision making, 19
declare, 63, 70
dedication, 79
defeated, 69
deliverance, 16, 33
delivered, 40, 51
demeanor, 12
demons, 8, 66
den, 68
Depression, 70
desert, 9
destiny, 7, 12, 31, 32, 33, 34, 39, 41, 44
Destiny, 29, 33

destroy, 51, 71
destruction, 56
development, 12
devil, 29, 40, 64, 66, 73
Devil, 7, 34, 40
directions, 1, 53
disappointed, 31
discern, 13, 53
discernment, 8, 14, 16
disciples, 5
Discipleship, 1
discipline, 62
distracted, 9, 56
distraction, 25
distress, 74
division, 25, 46, 56
Division, 46
dogs, 53
doors, 6, 9, 10, 18, 21, 25, 30, 33, 34
double jeopardy, 8
doubt, 2, 70
doves, 5
dreams, 61
dropping, 50
dry places, 20
ducks, 68

E

earth, 6, 7, 8, 9, 10, 17, 19, 29, 32, 36, 38, 42, 43, 46, 47, 49, 61, 62, 63, 72, 73, 75
earthquake, 21, 45
economy, 74

Edom, 33
education, 75, 78, 79
Egyptians, 33
Elijah, 44, 45
Emerging, 1
emotion, 25
emotions, 37
employees, 69
employment, 18, 19
empower, 30
encounter, 21
encourage, 30, 65, 78
encouragement, 30, 66, 80
ending, 40
enemy, 8, 9, 23, 24, 25, 33, 39, 40, 51, 54, 55, 57, 60, 64, 65, 66, 68, 72, 73, 77
entertainment, 74
envy, 45
Esther, 15, 68
eternal, 1, 10, 15, 76
evil, 4, 8, 33, 38, 41, 76
exaltation, 30
excuses, 10
expectation, 8, 62
eye, 24, 52

F

faith, 2, 14, 15, 16, 18, 19, 20, 26, 27, 30, 42, 44, 49, 50, 51, 52, 68, 69, 72, 79
Faith, 14, 15, 26, 30, 44, 72
faithful, 2, 32, 33, 42, 45, 59
faithfulness, 62

Fall, 35
family, 15, 18, 68, 79
famines, 58
fast food, 75
favoritism, 26
fear, 1, 8, 37, 38, 39, 44, 67, 68, 69, 77
fears, 37
fertile ground, 60, 63
fertility, 76
field, 47, 78
finisher, 40
fire, 4, 8, 45
First Lady Dr. Georgia Webb, 79
five-fold ministry, 48
flame, 24
flavor, 2
flesh, 1, 4, 9, 19, 25, 27, 32, 36, 38, 64, 65, 68, 72
flourish, 2, 17
foolish, 33
forbearance, 62
force, 25, 27
forgiveness, 24
forgotten, 4, 5, 27, 49, 50
forsaken, 9, 49
foundation, 20, 45, 48, 80
freedom, 68, 69
Freedom, 10
fruitful, 29
frustrated, 49
frustration, 14
future, 2, 4, 6, 7, 39, 42, 43, 47, 49, 62, 70, 77

G

game, 34, 65, 66, 67, 75
garden, 11, 41
gas tank, 2
generation, 6, 10, 15, 58, 76
gentleness, 62
giants, 33
gifts, 3, 23, 30
globe, 67
glory, 10, 19, 30, 31, 42
goats, 10
God, 1, 2, 3, 4, 5, 6, 7, 8, 9, 10, 11, 12, 13, 14, 15, 16, 19, 20, 21, 22, 23, 24, 25, 26, 27, 29, 30, 31, 32, 33, 34, 36, 37, 38, 39, 40, 41, 42, 43, 44, 45, 46, 47, 48, 49, 50, 51, 52, 53, 54, 55, 56, 57, 58, 59, 60, 61, 62, 63, 64, 65, 66, 67, 68, 69, 70, 71, 72, 73, 74, 75, 76, 77, 78, 79
good, 4, 9, 10, 12, 23, 29, 31, 33, 37, 39, 40, 42, 46, 54, 56, 61, 62, 64, 67, 74
goodness, 30, 62, 71
gospel, 24, 29, 76
government, 75
grace, 6, 20, 26, 30, 41, 46, 58, 72, 80
graveyard, 61
greater, 7, 10, 41, 51, 58, 76
groom, 27
growth, 12, 24, 27, 43, 48, 62, 65, 79

H

hades, 40
hair, 60, 76
harvest, 3, 61, 62
Healer, 26
healing, 16, 21, 73, 74, 75, 77

health, 47, 48, 49, 71, 76, 78
Healthcare workers, 18
healthy, 24, 66
heart, 4, 15, 23, 24, 26, 27, 32, 34, 47, 50, 65, 66, 68, 73
heat, 45, 62
heaven, 17, 49, 76
Heaven, 10, 29, 32, 43, 51, 52, 60, 63
heavens, 17, 36
hell, 37, 39, 40, 54
Hell, 40
Holy Spirit, 6, 7, 8, 9, 30, 42, 70
hope, 10, 19, 42, 44
horses, 1
hostage, 39, 68
hour, 1, 2, 4, 25, 26, 33, 34, 42, 43, 45, 48, 52, 55, 59
hourglass, 2, 4
households, 75
humble, 7, 76
humility, 7, 37
hungry, 1, 25

I

idolatry, 74
impairment, 69
impossible, 71
incarcerated, 19
incorruptible seed, 62
increase, 63
infected, 74
inheritance, 10
injustice, 74
Injustice, 9

inseparable, 16
inspiring, 80
intercession, 25, 73
Internal Battling, 48
intimidation, 69
invisible creature, 8
Israel, 33, 34, 53

## J

jail cell, 10
jealousy, 45
Jesus, 4, 5, 6, 7, 8, 9, 10, 12, 15, 26, 29, 31, 37, 38, 39, 40, 41, 43, 48, 54, 59, 60, 66, 67, 69, 70, 71, 73, 75, 76, 77, 78
John the Baptist, 43
Joseph, 51
journey, 45, 49, 52
joy, 13, 14, 62, 74

## K

kernel, 59
keys, 6, 30, 40
kill, 7, 34, 44, 45, 58, 60, 62, 68, 71
kindness, 62
Kingdom, 1, 3, 5, 6, 9, 14, 16, 29, 34, 43, 45, 47, 48, 54, 58, 66, 68, 69, 70, 77, 78
knowledge, 30, 48, 53, 75

## L

laborers, 3
lamp, 23, 24

landmarks, 31
lazy, 54
Leaders, 20
legs, 60
level, 14, 30, 31, 48
Liar, 7
light, 8, 20, 23, 24, 28, 41, 60, 63, 68
lightning strikes, 20
Lord, 3, 10, 16, 17, 32, 33, 34, 41, 46, 54, 56, 57, 59, 63, 66, 68, 70, 71
love, 2, 25, 27, 38, 42, 48, 53, 58, 59, 62, 66, 74, 75, 77

M

manifestation, 3, 8, 15, 62
manifestations, 8, 39
manna, 65
market, 5, 56
meal, 6
mentalities, 9
mercy, 20, 27, 30, 58
microwave, 65
mind, 2, 4, 12, 15, 23, 24, 41, 50, 60, 61, 64, 69, 77
mindset, 12, 14, 69
ministries, 54
mirror, 9
mission, 1, 3, 6, 9, 58, 78
Mission Radio Show, 78
Missouri, 78, 79
mistakes, 6, 36, 44, 64
momentum, 72
money, 74, 75
morning, 2, 72, 74
motivation, 7

motives, 19
mountain, 19, 20, 43, 69
mouth, 13, 17, 36, 44, 70
mouthpiece, 16
Mt. Calvary Powerhouse Church, 79

N

nails, 73
nation, 72, 74, 76
natural world, 1
neighbor, 55
new revelation, 12
New Testament, 43
night, 4, 8, 50, 62

O

obedience, 16, 30, 34, 37, 44
obedient, 15, 57
obstacles, 6
offense, 74
oil, 68, 75
ointment, 76
Old Testament, 8, 43
omega, 40
operation, 8, 25, 77
Opioid Epidemics, 9
opportunity, 41, 45, 61
oppress, 24, 25
Oppression, 70
outcast, 71
outdoors, 79

## P

pain, 36, 44, 62
painful, 3
pale horse, 58
pandemic, 2, 3, 18, 25, 32, 72
paralyze, 69
Pastors, 20
patience, 46
patty cake, 55
Paul, 22, 38
peace, 33, 58, 62, 77
permanent effect, 21
Peter, 30, 39
pews, 49
physician, 13
picture, 19, 61
pitcher, 64
plagues, 58
plans, 34, 41, 47, 50, 51, 68
plants, 63
playground, 65, 67, 68
possession, 33
power, 3, 7, 8, 9, 21, 24, 25, 29, 30, 40, 44, 63, 66, 67, 73, 74, 77, 79, 80
praise, 5, 50
pray, 46, 53, 55, 66, 74, 76
prayer, 3, 23, 31, 32, 37, 67
prayers, 18, 59
preparation, 27, 30, 34, 76
price, 51
principles, 3, 19, 24, 45, 66

prison, 18, 19, 21
problem, 13, 14, 53, 55, 66, 75
problems, 16, 47
procrastination, 62
programs, 19
promised land, 21
promises, 1, 9, 10, 54, 66, 70
Promotion, 30
prophecy, 13, 14, 15, 16, 20, 42, 43, 44, 53, 76
prophesy, 30
prophetic injunction, 4
prophetic reconstruction, 3, 24, 38
prospering, 21
prosperity, 62
protection, 54
provoke, 42, 43, 46
purpose, 3, 4, 9, 10, 17, 26, 29, 30, 34, 36, 39, 43, 47, 49, 61, 62, 65, 66, 68, 74

## Q

quarantined, 18

## R

Racism, 9
radio station, 31
rainbows, 17
reality, 8, 36, 37, 38, 39, 40, 48
rebellious, 74
rebuild, 20, 27, 51, 72
rebuilding, 3, 4, 5, 7, 10, 19, 38
reconstruct, 72

reconstruction, 3, 4, 6, 7, 8, 9, 11, 38, 64
recovery, 18, 41, 47, 48, 79
red horse, 58
redemption, 10
redirection, 21
Rejection, 21
Remnants, 1, 3, 11, 27, 37, 56
repent, 24, 55, 76
repentance, 76, 77
reposition, 72
resources, 2, 19, 80
responsibilities, 66
restore, 71
restructuring, 7, 10
resubmission, 64
revelation, 14, 16, 42, 75
revisions, 61
revival, 23, 24
Revivalist, 78
righteous, 2, 9, 59
righteousness, 59, 70
Road to Damascus, 37
rope, 49, 50, 52
royal, 15

S

sacrifice, 13
safe, 55
saints, 9, 29, 46
salvation, 29, 37, 41, 51
Samaritan, 75
Satan, 7, 8, 9, 40, 56, 62, 64, 66

Saul, 37, 38, 45, 46
schools, 75, 79
season of restoration, 13
Seasonal prophecy, 14
secrets, 3
security, 1
seeds, 59
seedtime, 62
self-control, 62
seminars, 79
serve, 10, 30, 51, 55
shield, 64
shortcomings, 9
Shout, 7, 40
sick, 13, 72
sickness, 13, 40
Silas, 22
sin, 9, 31, 41, 71, 76, 79
Single mothers, 18
sinners, 13
sisters, 27, 38, 67
soak, 15
social media, 44
soil, 12, 60
soldiers, 4, 45, 64
solitude, 60
soul, 24, 57, 66
speaking engagements, 80
spice, 2
spirit, 3, 4, 24, 25, 30, 36, 48, 50, 69, 70, 74, 77
Spirit, 1, 6, 7, 8, 9, 10, 11, 14, 15, 23, 24, 26, 27, 30, 31, 38, 42, 43, 48, 52, 54, 60, 62, 63, 65, 66, 67, 68, 69, 70, 72, 74, 77
Spiritual Motivator, 78

spiritual realm, 23
Spiritual Revelation, 34
Spiritual Warfare, 3, 64
spiritually, 1, 8, 13, 14, 21, 24, 25, 26, 27, 48, 50, 51, 64, 74
sports, 74, 75
Spring, 35
stagnant, 36, 37
star, 43
steal, 7, 71
stock markets, 74
storehouses, 66
strategy, 6, 46, 61
streets, 27
strength, 1, 16, 20, 37, 41, 44, 50, 64, 66
stuck, 41, 55, 67, 68
Submit, 64
success, 33, 34, 48, 61
suicide, 70
Suicide, 9, 79
summer, 62
Summer, 35
Sunday, 6, 51, 79
supernatural, 47, 72
support, 18, 19
surrender, 13, 21, 24, 26, 36, 62, 76
swing, 64, 65, 67, 68
sword, 57
system, 18, 19

T

tabernacle, 10
tactics, 65, 73

teach, 6, 18, 30
tear, 11, 41
tears, 21, 76
temple, 5
temporary, 21, 26, 54, 62, 67
temporary cause, 21
territory, 20, 54, 55
testimony, 12, 38
thirsty, 1
thoughts, 17, 39, 68
toxic, 61, 69
toxic relationships, 61
toxins, 74
train, 57
transformation, 3, 21, 32, 38, 60
transition, 3, 19, 21, 32, 68, 73
trauma, 18, 48
travel, 25
treasure, 1, 7, 41, 55
trial, 11, 41
trials, 59, 80
tribulations, 59, 80
triumph, 11, 41
trumpet, 57
truth, 2, 9, 16, 37, 48, 60, 77

U

unbelief, 2, 16
unemployed, 18
unemployment, 74
unfaithful, 32
unhappy, 68

unhealthy, 24
unity, 46, 56, 79
unveiling, 8-9
upset, 55

V

vacation, 15
valley, 19, 20, 23, 38, 69
vessel, 3
victim, 19, 40
Victory, 8
visible creature, 8
vision, 3, 13, 16, 49, 67, 68, 72
visions, 61
voice, 2, 32, 37, 42, 44, 56

W

Walmart, 25
war, 33, 34, 58, 65, 68
warn, 53, 56, 57, 58
Washington, 57
watchman, 53, 56, 57, 58
weak, 22, 74
weaker, 60
Wednesday, 6, 51
weeping, 13, 14, 74
weighed down, 55
wellness, 47
whiskey, 40
whisper, 13, 45
white horse, 58

winds, 20
wineskins, 12
winter, 62
Winter, 35
wisdom, 4, 7, 33, 68
wise, 34, 41
witness, 12
wolves, 54
womb, 9, 60
workforce, 18
world, 1, 2, 7, 9, 15, 18, 19, 26, 27, 34, 54, 55, 61, 64, 72, 74, 75, 77, 78, 79
worship, 5, 25
wounds, 71, 73, 75, 76
wrinkles, 60
wrong, 24, 55, 61, 76

Y

yoke of slavery, 40

Z

Zeal, 5
Zion, 36, 57, 71
zone, 72

www.ingramcontent.com/pod-product-compliance
Lightning Source LLC
LaVergne TN
LVHW012001070526
838202LV00054B/4991